John Lovell

The medical and surgical history of the Canadian North-West Rebellion of 1885

As told by members of the hospital staff corps

John Lovell

The medical and surgical history of the Canadian North-West Rebellion of 1885
As told by members of the hospital staff corps

ISBN/EAN: 9783742833259

Manufactured in Europe, USA, Canada, Australia, Japa

Cover: Foto ©ninafisch / pixelio.de

Manufactured and distributed by brebook publishing software
(www.brebook.com)

John Lovell

The medical and surgical history of the Canadian North-West Rebellion of 1885

THE

MEDICAL AND SURGICAL HISTORY

OF THE

CANADIAN

NORTH-WEST REBELLION

OF

1885,

AS TOLD BY MEMBERS OF THE HOSPITAL STAFF CORPS.

Montreal:
PRINTED BY JOHN LOVELL & SON.
1886.

REPORT OF THE SURGEON GENERAL.

OTTAWA, 13th May, 1886.

To the Honorable the MINISTER OF MILITIA AND DEFENCE.

SIR,

When on the first of April of last year (1885), in response to your invitation to me, I undertook the organization of a Medical Staff Corps I was not blind to the difficulties of the situation. There was no fixed Departmental Medical Staff, no Field Hospital or Ambulance Service, no organized Corps of Nurses, no fixed method of recognizing such societies as the St. John's Hospital Aid Society, the Red Cross, and other similar charitable associations.

Added to these the hurried levy, the necessarily scanty equipment of many of the men consequent upon this, the severity of the weather, the difficulties of transport, exposure of the Troops to the frost and snow in open cars, the long distances to be traversed through the gaps between the finished and unfinished portions of the railway, the difficulties of communication, the distance between this city, the base of supply, and the field of operations, the Major-General Commanding having already left Winnipeg for the front with a portion of the Troops,—all conspired to render the task one of unusual difficulty. Five or six regiments and two batteries, comprising the Ontario and Quebec and Nova Scotia contingents, were already on the march and were provided with, some of them at least, but very meagre or ill-regulated medical supplies and very few medical comforts. Under such circumstances, to provide attendance and comforts for the sick and the wounded, should unfortunately a collision occur between the Troops and the Half-breeds and Indians, as unfortunately did occur, appeared to be almost a hopeless task. Should any precaution be omitted or any article, no matter of how trifling a character, be unprovided, I felt that I should be exposed to the severest criticism, and your Department held responsible for any of my shortcomings. Nevertheless, I felt that there should be no hesitancy: the flower of our youth was under arms,—no care too great could be taken of them by the Medical Department, nor should any expense be spared in securing for them everything that could contribute to their health, their comfort and their safety; and I may now safely affirm that, whilst not extravagant, every means within the power of the Department were used to secure these ends. Matters, too, were complicated by the absence from the city of Dr. Douglas, V. C., to whom had been entrusted the preparation of Medical Supplies. Until after consultation with him, ignorant of what steps he had taken to carry out your orders, I was not in a position until the evening of Saturday, the fourth of April, to satisfactorily perfect the arrangements which I proposed to make. In the meantime I placed myself in communication with Colonel A. H. Girard of New York and Mr. Samuel Coulson of Montreal, who at my request consented to act as my purchasing agents in those cities.

Dr. Douglas returned upon the fourth, and placed in my hands a list of the drugs, instruments and surgical appliances which he had ordered at Montreal. On the evening of that day also, Drs. Roddick, of Montreal, and Sullivan, of Kingston, whom I had summoned by wire, reported to me here, and I put before them my views as to the necessities of the situation, and they accepted the positions, which, upon my recommendation, you had been pleased to approve should be offered to them. During the night I prepared a list, summary of which is attached hereto, of all that I believed to be necessary for the complete and thorough equipment of the Field-Hospitals, and on the following morning, Sunday, transmitted it by mail to my agent, Mr. Coulson, with instructions to procure and forward all to Winnipeg by express train, without an hour's delay, to the end that the Field Hospital Staff, with complete hospital equipment, might overtake the Major-General and his command—they were then a week in advance—before they crossed the Saskatchewan, and before a collision should occur with the enemy.

Too much credit cannot be given to Mr. Coulson for the manner in which he executed the order.

Cots, mattresses, sheets, pillows, and other articles of the kind required for the Field Hospitals were not in the market, and had to be manufactured to order. They were put in hand on the same day, (Sunday) and on Wednesday, the eighth, the complete equipment of Number One Field Hospital was shipped by car attached to mail train, and reached Winnipeg on the morning of the Tuesday following.

The equipment of Field Hospital No. 2 was despatched within a few days after; and the reserve supplies early in the following week.

Much of the equipment of the Field Hospitals it was found necessary to obtain from New York, and I must here gratefully acknowledge the rapidity and accuracy with which Col. Girard filled my orders, and forwarded everything required from that city for No. 1 Hospital, so as to reach Montreal in time to be shipped upon the same train with the stores from that city.

Let me mention here that the equipment of each Field Hospital was divided as nearly as possible into four equal parts, each part in itself forming a complete equipment for an hospital of 50 beds. The hospital accommodation provided was calculated for an army of 6000 men, and for a campaign of six months. Although the number of the men in the field exceeded this number by more than 1000, the sudden collapse of the rebellion after the battle of Batoche and the surrender of Big Bear left a large portion of the supplies on hand, the perishable portion of which was at once disposed of, and the remainder retained and turned into store—some of it for future use, and some of it handed over for the use of the Mounted Infantry School at Winnipeg.

Of the large quantity of goods returned into store, the greater portion was of the invoice of Messrs. Lyman, Sons & Co. of Montreal. Nearly all the packages had been broken, and therefore were not so valuable, and much that had been exposed to the air was worthless. These goods I sold back to that firm at a discount of fifty per cent., excepting the instruments purchased from them, which I returned to them at the original invoice price.

Previous to the return of Dr. Douglas, and on the morning following the date of your instructions, I had the honor to recommend the appointment of a Medical Staff, the establishment of two Field Hospitals, an Ambulance Corps, a Purveyor's

Department, and the framing of rules and regulations for the employment of nurses, whether voluntarily serving without pay, or as a hired staff.

I also recommended that the offers of service made by the Grey Nuns and other religious orders of the Roman Catholic Church, and of Protestant ladies throughout the country, as nurses, be accepted, and that the aid of the public generally be invited in the formation of Red Cross, St. John's Hospital and other societies whose object is the care and relief of the sick and the wounded, and, the providing of medical comforts such as could not well be provided by the Department.

Medical Staff.—In the memorandum I had the honor to submit I recommended, the more effectually to carry out the objects enumerated above, that a Medical Staff should be constituted, as follows, under the authority of paragraph 32 of the Regulations and Orders of the Militia of Canada, 1883 :

1. A Medical Director-General, to be the sole responsible, administrative head of the Medical Department, of the same rank and with the same powers and pay as the Director-General of the Medical Department of the British Army.

2. A Deputy-Surgeon General, with head-quarters in the field, to have, subject to the control of the Director-General, the superintendence and charge of all hospitals, ambulances, surgeons, nurses, and purveyors and such Red Cross or other societies as may be authorized by you. For the more effectual discharge of these duties, I directed him to report to the Major-General Commanding in the field, as well as, from time to time, to myself for your information. It to be part of his duty, and not the least important part of it, to advise, through the Major-General or other officer in command of the Troops, on all sanitary matters pertaining to, hospitals, camps, clothing, rations, drills, marches, etc., his powers, rank and pay to be the same as those of officers holding similar positions in Her Majesty's service.

Purveyor-General.—The Purveyor-General to have the sole charge, at his head-quarters, of the hospital marquees, or buildings and the surroundings, and to be responsible for their condition ; to inspect them frequently and to remove any defects which he might discover. He to have full charge of all stores for the use of the Field Hospitals and ambulances, of all the drugs and medicines, medical and surgical appliances, and, upon requisition duly made and countersigned by the Deputy Surgeon-General, to issue such as may be required to fill deficiencies in the Field Hospitals and ambulances, or Regimental Hospitals. To this officer, as well as to the Deputy Surgeon-General or Surgeon-Major in command of each Field Hospital, full instructions as to his and their duties were forwarded, copies of which I have the honor to attach hereto.

All of these recommendations, with one exception, you were pleased to approve. You preferred that the head of the Staff should have the rank of Surgeon-General, and in the Canada *Gazette* of Saturday, 25th April, under the head of Militia General Orders, is to be found the following :—

The following temporary medical appointments have been made, and Field Hospitals organized in connection with the force now on duty in the North-West territories :—

MEDICAL STAFF.

To be Surgeon-General :
  Darby Bergin, M.D., M.P., of Cornwall, Ont.
To be Deputy Surgeon-General.
  Thomas G. Roddick, M.D., of Montreal, Que.
To be Purveyor :
  Hon. Michael Sullivan, M.D., of Kingston, Ont.

HOSPITAL AND AMBULANCE CORPS.

FIELD HOSPITAL NO. I.

To be Surgeon Major :
  Campbell Mellos Douglas, V. C., late Deputy Surgeon-General H. M.'s Service.
To be Surgeons :
  Dr. James Bell, of Montreal, Que.
  Dr. Edward A. Gravely, of Cornwall, Ont.
  Dr. J. Roddick, of Winchester, Ont.
  Dr. E. Hooper, of Kingston, Ont.
  Dr. Fred. Hamilton Powell, of Ottawa, Ont.

FIELD HOSPITAL NO. 2.

To be Surgeon-Major :
  Dr. Henry Raymond Casgrain, of Windsor, Ont.
To be Surgeon :
  Dr. R. Tracy, of Belleville, Ont.
  Dr. N. O. Walker, of Toronto, Ont.
  Dr. Francis Murray, of Montreal, Que.
  Dr. Cloutier, of St. Arsène, Que.
  Dr. Philippe Pelletier, of Quebec, Que.

The Deputy Surgeon-General.—In the selection of Dr. Roddick, as Chief of the Medical Staff in the Field, I had an eye solely to the efficient performance of the duties, to give confidence to the country that the best medical and surgical skill was at the head of the service—that all was done, humanly speaking, that could be done for the comfort and the safety of our young men in the North-West, and I am glad to say that his appointment gave the greatest satisfaction and inspired universal confidence. One of the most distinguished of Canadian Surgeons, young, full of vigor, of powerful physique, knowing no fatigue, a first-class horseman, I looked upon him as just the man for the place, and the result, as shewn by the letters of our sick and wounded who were under his care, and of the Press, which is never slow to detect error or mismanagement—and equally ready, I must say, to offer a generous meed of praise, where found to be due—has amply justified his selection and stamped approval upon his work.

The Purveyor-General.—Hardly second in importance to the Deputy-Surgeon General was the officer to whom was to be trusted the control of the supplies, and of the comforts provided for the hospitals. Upon him was to depend the careful, economical, and the honest distribution of the large quantities of stores to be committed to his charge. Experience in camps of instruction and in frontier service, long taught me that there was little limit to the wants and to the demands of Regimental Surgeons for medical and other supplies. The opinion prevailed among them that, so long as stores were provided by the Government, they were at liberty to requisition for them, almost without curb or restraint; and the result was a wasteful and, shall I say it, an extravagant misappropriation of the public property. To check and to prevent such waste and such misappropriation required at the head of this branch of the service a man with a thorough knowledge of its wants and of its requirements, who knew what to give and what to refuse—what was necessary equally for a Surgeon in charge of a Detachment or a Regiment. Such a man I found in the Hon. Dr. Sullivan, Professor of Surgery, Royal College of Surgeons, Kingston. To him I offered the position of Purveyor-General, and it gives me great satisfaction to say that he filled it with credit to himself and to the great advantage of the country. He was emphatically the right man in the right place. He knew when to say no, and had the courage then to say it.

Orderlies and Dressers.—In addition to physicians and surgeons, Field Hospitals required dressers, orderlies and nurses, and there being no Ambulance Corps, or trained bearer companies, it was necessary to provide them on the instant. I was aware that in some of the medical schools, during the past year or two, more or less attention had been given to ambulance work, and at Montreal and Toronto lessons in First Aid and Stretcher Drill had been given, and classes formed by Dr. Bell, of McGill College, and Dr. O'Reilly, surgeon to the Toronto General Hospital, and other surgeons of that city. Upon its being made known that I would accept volunteers for this work, almost every medical student in the Dominion, without exception, volunteered his service, showing a spirit worthy of the highest praise, asking only as remuneration that he be sent to the front free of transport expense. I accepted the services of as many of these young gentlemen as I possibly could, without entailing too great outlay ; but I recommended that in no case should service be accepted without pay. It was manifest to me that the Hospitals, to be of real benefit to the sick and to the wounded, must be under the most perfect discipline, and experience teaches that where men are employed in any service which is voluntary, and to which no pay is attached, they feel under very little restraint, and are not inclined to practice the virtue of obedience, beyond what it may please them at the moment to observe. So many having volunteered as dressers, orderlies, stretcher-bearers, or helpers in any capacity, in the field or in the hospitals, I requested Dr. Fenwick, the eminent Professor of Surgery of McGill College, Montreal, to select the number necessary for one Field Hospital, from the graduating class, and the third and second year students of his University. Dr. O'Reilly of Toronto was kind enough to make the selection for the other Hospital from the similar classes in that city. Many of these young men did noble work, regardless of danger. Where the bullets fell thickest, with a heroism that has never been exceeded, they were to be found, removing the wounded and the dying to places of shelter and of safety in the rear. Some cases of individual heroism are reported to me, which I feel call for more than a passing remark ; and embolden me to say that amongst these non-combatant lads, and the Staff to which they belonged, are to be found some of the greatest heroes of the war. At Batoche I am told that during the fight a flag was thrust from the window of the church, and was observed by a surgeon and a student who were under shelter from the fire at a couple of hundred yards distance. The student immediately he perceived it proposed that a party should at once go to the relief of the one demanding succor.

No one appeared willing to second his proposal. To go to the church through the open under such a terrible fire as was being poured from the Half-breed pits, seemed to be like proceeding to certain death ; but persisting, the surgeon said, " if you are determined to go and we can find two volunteers to assist us in carrying a stretcher I am with you." Two men from the Grenadiers of Toronto at once stepped forward ; and the four started upon their perilous journey—crawling upon their bellies —taking advantage of any little inequality of ground to cover them, and to shield them from the bullets of the Half-breeds. They reached the church—the bullets tearing up the earth all around them—without a scratch, and, breathing a short prayer for their deliverance thus far from death and danger, they looked around for him whom they had risked, and were still risking, their lives, to succor and to save. They found him in the person of a venerable priest, who had been wounded in the thigh, and they at once proceeded to remove him, after administering temporary aid. To remain in the church was to court certain death. To return to their corps seemed to be no less perilous; but they chose the latter. When they sortied from the church, so astonished were the Half-breeds at their daring that they ceased their fire for a moment. This time, returning, they had no cover, and were obliged to march erect. Bullets flew thick and fast; but the condition of the wounded man precluded anything like hurry, and they hastened slowly. God watched over them and protected them, and they reached their comrades in safety—their wounded charge also escaping without further harm. Such conduct deserves recognition, and I beg respectfully to call attention to it in this official way. I have not yet been able to obtain the names of the two noble fellows belonging to the Grenadiers, but I hope this notice of it will bring the information I desire. The other two are Surgeon Gravely of No. 1 Field Hospital, and Mr. Norris Worthington, from the same Hospital.

The manner in which Capt. Mason was rescued and brought in by, I believe, Dr. Codd of the 90th and one of the young dressers was an exhibition of marked courage by members of the Medical Staff. Other instances well deserving of commendation have been reported to me, and I would respectfully suggest enquiry into all such cases, and, if they be found as reported to me, that honorable recognition of them be made.

Nurses.—Your invitation to the different religious orders, both Protestant and Catholic, and to ladies generally throughout the country, to volunteer as nurses to our brave youth who might unfortunately be the victims of disease, or of wounds received in battle, was promptly answered by communities and individuals from all parts of the Dominion. The Nuns, ever ready at the call of charity, placed themselves at your disposal as did the Sisters of St. John the Divine, belonging to the Church of England at Toronto, and ladies of the highest standing throughout the country, some of them trained under Florence Nightingale, many of them in the Hospitals of London and New York, offered their services, all without fee or reward. Nor was the offer of service as nurses confined to Canada. Many such offers came from ladies in the United States, begging to be permitted to share in the work of charity. Where so many offered to take part in the holy work it was difficult for me to choose, and I hesitated for a time before making a selection. It was not until the removal of the Base Hospital from Swift Current to Moosejaw, a more convenient and more healthful situation, to which Hospital all were remove from Saskatoon that could be moved with safety, that, with your approval I accepted the services of the Sisters of St. John the Divine of Toronto. Dr. Roddick, the Deputy Surgeon-General, and the Honorable Dr. Sullivan bear testimony to the value of their services and have for them nothing but praise. Dr. Boyd of London, who pronounced the hospitals at Saskatoon and Moosejaw to be the best equipped and best managed he ever saw, also adds his testimony in their favor. I must congratulate the Lady Superior upon the economical way in which she performed her work and of the careful management of the funds entrusted to her to cover the expenses of the return journey of herself and staff. Of the $200 confided to her for that purpose, she returned, if my memory serves me well, about $70. May I be permitted to suggest that a contribution towards the furnishing of their new Home at Toronto would be a graceful act, and would be appreciated and approved by the country.

Ladies' Aid Societies.—Before the first echo of the news of the Battle of Fish Creek, which had been flashed over the wires, had died away, offers to form St. John's Hospital Aid Societies and other similar Societies, came to me from all parts of the Dominion. The ladies of St. John's Church, Prescott, led the way, and were almost immediately followed by the ladies of Montreal, Toronto, London, Hamilton, and other places, proposing to furnish bandages, clothing, necessaries, medical comforts and even delicacies for the sick and the wounded. Under your instru · ions I directed that all such goods delivered to the Purveyor-General or his agent at Winnipeg would be forwarded to the parties to whom they were directed in the field, free of expense to the senders, by the Government Transport Corps. I regret to say that this system was not found to work well ; and I would recommend that in the future, should unfortunately this country be again engaged in war, all such medical comforts and supplies, whether furnished by Aid Societies to troops in the Field or by individuals to their friends serving in the army, should be undertaken by an association or a society formed expressly for that purpose. I would also recommend—the experience of the late campaign having shewn that large quantities of useless material were forwarded—that every package should be opened, inspected, all that was useless withdrawn, and only that which was of value repacked and forwarded. It is manifest that this duty is not one for the Government, and should be confided to private civil associations. Much of the material, collected after much labor and at great cost, never reached the poor fellows for whom it was intended, was stolen by the way, plundered, I am ashamed to say by the teamsters, and some, as we are informed, fell into the hands of Poundmaker and his braves, who for some days feasted gloriously upon potted meats, preserved fruits, marmalades and jellies ; and held high carnival with the fine brandies and luscious wines intended for the brave fellows shut up in Battleford.

Red Cross Corps.—The suggestion to invite the formation of a Red Cross Corps was promptly met; and, with your approval, I accepted the offer of Mr. Edwin Wragge, Local General Manager of the Grand Trunk Railway at Toronto, to organize a Red Cross Corps in that city, and authorized the formation of one by him, whose duty it was to be to look after the sick and the wounded, in the field, and who were to undergo instruction in First Aid and Stretcher Drill during the week previous to their departure for the front under the direction of Dr. Nattress of Toronto. This drill consisted of lifting up into and lifting from the ambulance in such a manner as not to injure or cause discomfort to the wounded, and of placing them on and removing them from the stretchers; the proper method of stretcher-bearing, and of removing them from the stretchers to the beds in the hospitals; they were also instructed in the proper methods of arresting hemorrhage, of bandaging, of setting fractures and of giving temporary relief and assistance until the aid of the Surgeons in the rear or in the hospitals could be obtained.

The gentlemen belonging to this Corps were almost without exception young medical men, graduates in medicine and surgery, who performed the duty without pay. They were provided with transport and rations at the expense of the Government, and upon their arrival at Swift Current were ordered to Battleford, and there placed under the command of Brigade-Surgeon Strange, arriving at that point, almost immediately after the battle of Cut Knife; under the direction of that officer, they rendered valuable service in the Hospital there.

Wines and Spirits.—Anticipating that, through the mistaken kindness of friends in the older Provinces, quantities of wines and spirits would be forwarded with the supplies and comforts, I directed that, under no circumstances, should such be forwarded to the Troops in the field. That wines and spirits could only be allowed for hospital use, and, if forwarded to the Purveyor, would be confiscated by him, placed in the hospital stores employed for no other purpose than for the sick, and then only upon requisition made by the Surgeon in charge of the Hospital, who would be held responsible therefor; and in any case, where the Purveyor was of opinion that the quantity asked for was in excess of the requirements he was directed to issue no more than, in his opinion, was really necessary, reporting his refusal and reasons therefor, to the Deputy Surgeon-General for the information of the Major-General Commanding.

Recommendations.—Having thus briefly sketched the operations of the Medical Staff in the field, I may be permitted to direct attention to that which I consider to be the especial weakness of the service—I mean the regimental system. During the late campaign it was found to be expensive, extravagant and almost unmanageable. With the exception, I think, of two or three corps, the Queen's Own, the Grenadiers and the Seventh Battalion, no Regimental Surgeon accompanied his regiment to the front. The Sixty-fifth, the Ninth, the Halifax Battalion, the Montreal Garrison Artillery, and others from the older Provinces, all took with them Volunteer Surgeons, and, with the exception of the Halifax Battalion, not one of them—of the Surgeons attached for the campaign—has made a satisfactory report of the cases treated by him or of the sanitary or unsanitary condition of his regiment that has reached me.

Surgeons recruited in an emergency—Regimental System.—Surgeons recruited in an emergency without any previous military medical training, are apt to be and as in some instances during the late campaign were found to be, very inefficient and, from their want of discipline and ignorance of military law, were very difficult of control, and gave no adequate service in return for the large amounts of money expended upon them for transport, pay and rations.

Medical Staff Corps.—I strongly recommend, therefore, that a Medical Staff Corps be formed, very much on the lines of the Medical Staff Corps of Her

Majesty's service, due regard being had to the differences of conditions and nature of the two services. The British Medical Service, being a permanent one, ours, so to speak, being more of a temporary charter, its component parts often varying, requently changing. The system which I propose includes an administrative and executive staff, Field Hospital Corps, Ambulance Corps and a Military Cadet Corps. From this latter, year by year, the Staff Surgeons to be drawn. In my opinion there should be a Surgeon-General, the administrative head of the service, a Deputy Surgeon-General in each of the Provinces of Ontario and Quebec, a Deputy Surgeon-General for the Maritime Provinces, a Deputy Surgeon-General for Manitoba, for the North-West Territories and British Columbia, one Brigade-Surgeon in each military district, one Surgeon-Major to each brigade division,—the present Regimental Surgeons, whilst not severing their connection entirely with their regiments, to be considered as Surgeons of the Staff so long as they remain within their brigade divisions. To meet the future requirements of the service, both for Surgeons of the Staff, Field Hospitals and Ambulance Corps, I beg to recommend that Medical Cadet Corps be established at the seats of our medical schools, say at Montreal, Toronto, Kingston, London, Halifax and Winnipeg; and thoroughly taught Ambulance and Field Hospital work. After graduation, having passed a satisfactory examination, they would be eligible as Surgeons of the Staff. During their pupilage they can be made available, should the necessity arise, as quarter-masters, assistant quarter-masters, hospital sergeants, hospital orderlies, dressers, etc. From them could be obtained also, if necessary, some of the material for bearer companies.

Before appointment as a Surgeon each candidate should be subjected to an examination, which should embrace the following subjects:

    a. Military surgery, including transport of sick and wounded.

    b. Military medicine and pathology and therapeutics.

    c. Military hygiene.

    d. Duties of executive medical officers, during peace and war.

He must also give evidence of having attended a complete' course of operative in some recognized Medical University; and, in the presence of the examiners, write a thesis upon some military medical or hygienic subject. All warrant officers should pass an examination such as is required by the medical regulations of Her Majesty's army. No Staff Surgeon should be promoted to the rank of Surgeon-Major until after ten years' service. No Surgeon-Major should be appointed to the rank of Brigade-Surgeon except on the grounds of ability and merit; and in accordance with the regulations laid down for the Medical Department of Her Majesty's Army.

The establishment of a Cadet Corps would entail some expense, but this would be trifling in comparison with the benefits to be derived, and if an annual allowance were made to the several Medical Universities, to enable them to give a full course each year, upon the subjects above mentioned, Canada would, in a few years, have as an efficient Medical Staff Corps as any country in the world. If possible, and I think it is, a Field Hospital should be attached to every camp of instruction and bearer companies should be formed in proportion to the strength of the brigade division. The camps of instruction, or as many of them as it be possible, should be inspected by the Surgeon-General or, in his absence, by the

Deputy Surgeon-General of the Province. The Surgeon-General should also inspect the Infantry School Barracks and Hospitals at least twice a year; should inform himself thoroughly as to their sanitary condition and as to the manner in which the Attending Surgeons perform their duties, and report thoroughly thereon, through the Major-General Commanding, for the information of the Honorable the Minister of Militia and Defence. This would entail some little expense, as it would occupy that officer probably 20 or 25 days in the year, but the country would reap a corresponding advantage.

Transport Service.—Owing to the long distances which had to be traversed between the Base Line and the Troops in the field, and the want of a Medical Transport Service, it was found very difficult to forward medical supplies to the various Hospitals, at Battleford, Calgary and Saskatoon, and to the head-quarters of the columns of the North West Field Force. To remedy this, I would recommend that each Military District be supplied with at least one hospital cart and in the event of active service one should be attached, with a Surgeon in charge, who should have under him one Apothecary and two Orderlies. One such cart, upon the model of the U. S. army cart, which will contain everything needful for a brigade, I have had constructed—a full description of which I send herewith. To each Field Hospital in each district there should be attached, at the least, six ambulance waggons; but, inasmuch as the strong express waggon, such as is used by the Express Companies in our cities, can be readily converted into ambulances; and as it is to be hoped that many years will elapse before necessity arises for their use, I do not recommend the construction of any at this moment. The few stores now on hand and not required for the use of the Infantry Schools I recommend to be sold. They consist principally of instruments, the greater number of which were purchased in New York at the contract price to the Purveyor's Department of the United States Army, which is much below the price at which surgeons can purchase them from the manufacturers; and I would recommend that medical men should have the opportunity of purchasing them out of store at the original cost price. There are also in store a large number of I. R. sheets, which were not used, are in perfect order, and might be sold on the same terms as the instruments. These sheets are white, finished on both sides, of the best material, and were obtained at a very great reduction upon the usual retail price.

The goods sent out by Her Royal Highness the Princess Louise, but which were not used because the Hospitals were already sufficiently supplied before their arrival, are now being distributed by you to the Hospitals and charities, which, in your opinion most need them, in accordance with Her Royal Highness' instructions ; and I take occasion here to express the gratitude, which I, in common with all loyal Canadians felt at this manifestation on her part, of her continued interest in the welfare of Canada and the Canadians.

I beg to bring to your notice the zeal and ability displayed by Mr. J. A. Polkinghorne, whom you assigned to my office. He was untiring in the performance of his duties, and deserves not only especial mention by me here, but adequate remuneration in the shape of extra pay, his work not having been limited to the ordinary office hours, but extending until two and three, and frequently four, o'clock of the morning.

Of the manner in which the Canadian Pacific Railway and the Grand Trunk

Railway managed their part of the Transport Service I cannot speak too highly. The former transported a car laden with medical stores from Montreal to Winnipeg, via Chicago, in six days and a few hours, and the latter railway in somewhat less than six days. A rapidity unprecedented.

The details of the several Hospitals will be found in the several reports of the Deputy Surgeon-General and Purveyor-General appended hereto; and I desire to express my high appreciation of the manner in which they performed their duties.

It would be ungrateful of me to close this report without most warmly thanking Purveyor General Baxter of the United States Army, who in the friendliest unofficial way, gave me the benefit of his large experience, supplying me with hints and suggestions that much facilitated me in the work so new to me, and enabled me to save large amounts of money to the country.

I append also a list of the Pension Boards.

I have the honor to be, Sir,

Your obedient servant,

D. BERGIN,

Surgeon-General, Canadian Militia.

13

(A).—INSTRUCTIONS TO DEPUTY SURGEON-GENERAL.

HEAD QUARTERS, MEDICAL STAFF, MILITIA OF CANADA,
OTTAWA, April 6th, 1885.

DR. RODDICK,
Deputy Surgeon-General, Montreal.

SIR,

As principal Medical Officer, upon your arrival at Qu'Appelle, or at the head-quarters of the General Commanding, you will, with the junction of the General at once, or at such time as may appear to him to be necessary, issue such instructions regarding sanitary precautions to be observed for protecting the health of the Troops as he may consider requisite for the guidance of the Medical Officers.

You had better appoint a Brigade Surgeon, with the approval of the General, who shall daily inspect the camp, and especially inform himself as to the health of the Troops, and of the appearance of any zymotic disease amongst them, and he shall immediately, on being informed of the appearance of any such disease, examine into the cause of the same, whether such disease proceed from or is aggravated by sanitary defects in the camp, bad or deficient water-supply, dampness, marshy ground, insufficient clothing, or from any local cause; or from bad food, intemperance, unwholesome liquors, fruit or want of shelter, too much exposure, fatigue, or any other cause, and report immediately to the Major-General Commanding, on such causes, and the immediate measures necessary for their removal, sending a copy of all such reports to the Medical Director General here, and report at least once daily on the progress or declining of the disease, and on the means adopted for the remo-val of its causes, until the disease shall have come to an end. You will at such intervals as I shall hereafter direct forward to me full information on all subjects, connected with the hygiene of the force, together with such recommendations for improving this service as you or the Brigade-Major may report to you to be requi-site. All Medical Officers in charge of Field Hospitals should transmit to you, for the guidance of your Brigade Sanitary Officer, full information as to the sanitary state of the Troops and the Hospitals, and on all matters affecting the health and physical efficiency of the men, at such intervals as I may from time to time direct.

You will direct the Sanitary Officers in the field, and the Surgeon-Major of each Field Hospital, to draw up a weekly sanitary report on the state of the Army, and of the hospitals, to be sent to you for the information of the General Commanding, a copy of which you will please transmit to me immediately upon its receipt.

Upon your arrival at the head-quarters of the Major General, and immediately after having reported yourself to him, ascertain the amount of transport that will be required for the sick, the nature and extent of the stores and supplies of all kinds necessary for such transport, and the number of Medical Officers and atten-dants that you may deem to be necessary.

You will be furnished from this office without delay with a detail of each Field hospital including the Surgeon-Major and Surgeons, Dressers and Dispensers. As all the Field Hospitals and the Purveyor's department are under your control and direction, you will make a special inspection of all the stores, medicines, drugs, medical comforts, beds, cots, bedding, utensils and arrangements for cooking. You will see that the stores and water-supply are good and sufficient; that there is a due proportion of Medical Officers according to the number and state of the sick, and that in case of the transport of the sick a sufficient number of Orderlies, at least one in every ten of the sick, is provided.

Should you discover any defects in any of the above particulars likely to affect injuriously the health of the Troops during their transport, you will forthwith report the same in writing to the General Commanding, and transmit copy of your report to the Brigade-Surgeon, and instruct him to forward the same with his remarks to this office.

You will be careful, when requisitions for instruments, surgical appliances and medical comforts are presented to you by Regimental or Detachment Surgeons, to ascertain beyond any doubt that necessity exists for the issue asked for, and that it is not in excess of the actual need or want of the regiment or detachment; and in all cases, when possible to obtain it, for anything beyond a small quantity which is of immediate urgency (in this you will use your discretion) you should obtain the signature of the Major-General Commanding.

I must ask you to use the telegraph wire as seldom as possible, and when using it to be most concise, so as to bring the expenditure of your department under that head to the lowest possible amount.

You will please advise me by letter immediately upon your arrival as to the health of the staff of the Field Hospital which you will take with you to-morrow morning from Montreal to headquarters.

The staff of Field Hospital No. 2 will follow you within a day or two.

The Purveyor, who will also have charge of the medicines, instruments and surgical appliances and medical comforts necessary for the use of the Troops in the North-West, will leave to-morrow night with his assistants, and, within a week or ten days at the furthest, will have a supply of all that is needed for the sick in the hospital or in the field, upon which you can draw by requisition whenever you may have occasion to do so.

I have the honor to be, Sir,

Your obedient servant,

D. BERGIN,
Medical Director-General.

(E.—INSTRUCTIONS TO PURVEYOR-GENERAL, HON. DR. SULLIVAN.

OTTAWA, April 10, 1885.

HON. DR. SULLIVAN,

Kingston, Ont.

SIR,

I have the honor to inform you that you have been appointed Purveyor to the Medical Branch of the Militia Department, and, until further orders, with head-quarters at Winnipeg, to which point you will proceed without any delay. Upon your arrival you will report by wire to the Major-General Commanding in the field, and you will be responsible to the Medical Officer in charge of the Troops in Manitoba and the North-West Territories, for the proper performance of your duties.

2. In all matters of discipline, you will be under the command of the Major-General, and you are bound to obey all orders issued by him, with reference to the duties of your department.

3. On all matters of importance connected with your duties, which do not admit of reference to me here, you will do well to address the Major-General Commanding, and obtain his opinion and advice. In all such instances, your reference will be made through the Medical Officer in charge, the Deputy Surgeon-General.

4. You will have the sole charge at Winnipeg, or at whatever point the Major-General Commanding may decide to fix the Base Hospital, of all buildings and surroundings, be responsible for their condition, inspect them frequently, at conve-nient hours, take instant steps to remove any defects which you may discover, or which may be brought to your notice by the Surgeon-Major Commanding the Hospital, or other inspecting officer.

5. Under you, steps must be taken for the cleanliness and order of the Hospital and its surroundings, and you will be responsible that they are kept in a perfectly cleanly state.

6. You will take care that the culinary arrangements for the Hospital are complete, that the cook and his assistants discharge their duties properly, that the cooking and all kitchen utensils are kept perfectly clean, that the patients' meals are properly prepared, and punctually served.

7. You will take every precaution to prevent any waste of fuel.

8. It will be your duty to see that the men employed in the kitchens are steady, cleanly, and instructed so as to make them efficient cooks after a short training. I shall endeavor to provide you with cookery books to aid you in this branch of your work.

9. You will report to the Deputy Surgeon-General from time to time the names of such of the assistant cooks, or of the hospital orderlies as, in your opinion, are fit to take charge as cooks of divisional hospitals, should such be established.

10. You will obtain every morning, from the Medical Officers in charge at Winnipeg, the name, regiment, rank, regimental number, and the date of admission, death or discharge, of every man treated in the Hospital.

11. You will be careful, on the admission of a soldier into the Hospital, to

receive over his pack, etc., and to enter a list of the contents thereof in a pack store check-book which you will keep for that purpose. The condition of the man's effects when received must be indicated on the face of the list by initial letters, thus : 'N' for new, 'G' for good, 'B' for bad, and 'W' for worn, and great care must be observed in registering the articles correctly, so that no dispute may arise on the discharge of the man from the Hospital. A duplicate list is to be prepared and handed to the ward-master, or other non-commissioned officer in charge. The pages of the check-books are to be numbered consecutively, and in the index the name of each man is to be entered in regimental order, the number of the pack being specified against his name. On his discharge he is to receive the pack from the pack store, on the production of the said duplicate, duly receipted.

12. The effects are to be carefully put up and arranged in shelves in the store, in numerical order, each pack bearing the number giving the list of its contents in the check-books, and in the counterfoils in the possession of the patient, or of the ward-master.

13. The packs are not to be placed on the racks too closely together, and the store is at all times to be kept dry and well ventilated.

14. You will on no account allow soiled linen or clothing to be placed in the packs or bundles. All such articles are to be thoroughly cleansed, and the expense charged against the battalion or regiment to which the man belongs.

15. To prevent errors, or exchanges, a clothing No., corresponding with that on the pack to which the linen, etc., belongs, is to be attached to each article sent to the wash, and, on their return from the wash, they are to be immediately placed in their respective packs.

16. You will keep a book in which you will cause to be entered every article which it may be found necessary to send to the wash from the pack store, with the name, regiment, etc., of the patient to which they belong, and the number by which his pack is distinguished in the store.

17. No access is to be allowed to the packs, nor are any articles to be delivered to the patients, except on the certificate of the Ward Orderly, approved by the Medical Officer in charge, that the article is absolutely necessary for the patient's use and comfort.

18. You will retain the effects of the deceased men until you receive orders regarding their disposal from the commanding officers of the battalions or regiments, to which they belong.

19. You will prepare all wills for the patients when required so to do, and you will be provided with forms for that purpose.

20. You will keep, for future reference, a correct register of all wills prepared by you.

21. You will, on the death of a patient in the Hospital, make all necessary funeral arrangements, if required by the Surgeon-Major in charge of the Hospital so to do, and you will give notice to the chaplain of the time of the burial.

22. You will report the deaths to the Commanding Officer of the battalion, regiment or battery to which the men belong.

23. You will keep an establishment book containing the names of all the officers and servants of every description belonging to the Hospital, with the dates of their appointment and removal, and the rates of their daily pay, rations, etc.

24. You will pay the wages of such of the Hospital servants as do not belong to the Hospital corps, and you will make requisition for the pay and allowances of the men belonging to that corps attached to the Hospital at Winnipeg.

25. Should you at any time require further assistance, you will apply to the Major-General Commanding, through the Deputy Surgeon-General, for non-commissioned officers or men belonging to the Troops in the field to be detailed for the purpose of acting as storekeepers or issuers. When men belonging to the Troops are not available, you may engage civilians, with the approval of the Major-General Commanding.

26. You will provide for the subsistence of the sick, and it will be your duty to countersign, all demands upon the contractors for supplies, and frequently to inspect articles upon delivery, both as to quantity and as to quality.

27. You will be held responsible for the cleanliness and order of the rooms or buildings in which the provisions are stored, and you will see that every precaution is taken to prevent injury to, or waste of the provisions, drugs, medical comforts, or other stores committed to your charge.

28. You will cause a book to be kept in which you will enter daily the receipts and expenditure for all articles of subsistence, and from this you will prepare, or cause to be prepared monthly returns, invariably taking stock on the last day of each month, in order to prove the accuracy of the remains in the said returns.

29. You will obtain as early as possible each day, not later than 12 o'clock, noon, from the non-commissed officer charged with the duty, a requisition for the extras prescribed for the day, and you will, on receipt of such requisition, as soon after as practicable, cause the articles to be issued.

30. You will, on receipt of requisition for diets required for each ward, or division, for the following day, cause to be prepared by your store keeper, a statement of the actual quantity of provisions to be issued for the diets of the day, which statement, after being examined by you, will be handed to the cook, to enable him to check the issue made by the storekeeper, and to regulate the messes for the Hospital.

31. At the end of each month, you will compare the requisitions and diet-sheets and stores issued, and report to the Deputy Surgeon-General any discrepancies that may be discovered. In the case of the death or discharge of the patient previous to the issue of the following day's diet, the ward orderly should be directed to send notice of the same to you, that you may stop the issue, and should the ward orderly neglect to give this notice, the stoppage will be charged to him.

32. You will bring to the notice of the Deputy Surgeon-General any instance in which it appears to you that an unusual amount of extras has been prescribed, or that an unusual course of exceptional dieting has been followed, and you will, at the same time, transmit the diet-sheets to that officer.

33. When necessary, and no other means of transport is provided, you will pay for the conveyance of the sick to the Hospital, but the sum so expended should be recovered from the Paymaster of the corps to which the men belong.

34. You will frequently inspect the Hospital, and ascertain that the stores are correct in number, and properly complete.

35. You will comply with the requisitions of the Medical officer in charge of the

B

Hospitals, or Divisional Hospitals, for articles included in the authorized schedule ; and in case of apparent extravagance in quantity or quality you will report the same to the Deputy Surgeon-General, in order that it may be brought under the notice of the Major-General Commanding.

36. You are not authorized to supply any article of diet or extras, or any hospital stores, not included in the schedule attached hereto, without the special sanction of the Deputy Surgeon-General.

37. You will frequently inspect the supplies delivered by the contractors, rejecting any articles not found equal to sample, and you will direct the immediate replenishment of the inferior article by one of a proper description, in default of which you will purchase the necessary supplies at the contractor's expense.

38. The steward of the Base Hospital at Winnipeg will furnish you daily with a requisition for the total amount of perishable articles required for the diet of the following day.

39. You will provide and keep up the furniture and utensils, and supply clothing, bedding, medical comforts, etc., in accordance with the schedule attached hereto.

40. You will make the necessary arrangements for washing the hospital clothing and bedding at Winnipeg, and for the repair of the same, either by local contract, or by the employment of work people by the day.

41. The following returns will be made to you by the surgeons in charge of field regimental detachment or Divisional Hospital, daily and monthly, as hereafter:

1st. A daily abstract of diets and extras, which you will forward to this department on the 1st and 16th of each month.

2nd. Monthly diet-sheets of patients under treatment, to be forwarded on the last day of the month.

3rd. A nominal return of admissions, discharges and deaths during the month, to be forwarded on the last day of the month.

You will carefully examine their returns and report on any large expenditure you may discover therein.

42. On receipt of bills for the supply of medicines, or for the purchase or repair of instruments, or for stores of any kind, you will prepare an abstract of the same, and transmit it to this Department, through the Deputy Surgeon-General.

43. You will be held responsible that the supplies for the hospitals are from time to time duly supplemented and kept up.

44. You will furnish, for the information and guidance of the Deputy Surgeon-General, the Surgeon-Major in charge of each hospital, and the Surgeons and Asst.-Surgeons attached to each battalion, regiment or battery, a copy of the list of stores to be obtained on requisition from you at Winnipeg.

45. You will consult with the principal Medical Officer as to the description of supplies which will be most probably required, and you will prepare estimates of the same, and forward them to me, with such observations as you may wish to make.

46. You will transmit to me, at the end of each month, a return showing the detailed receipts and issues for the month, indicating whence and from whom you

derived the supplies, to what hospitals, regiments, battalions, or batteries the issues have been made, upon the authority of whose requisitions, and the articles remaining in hand. You should also report to me therewith the quality of the articles supplied.

47. You will keep on hand, properly packed, a full supply of hospital stores for the establishment of Divisional Hospitals, upon requisitions for such supplies from the Deputy Surgeon-General.

48. As you will be held personally responsible that the wants of the hospitals are amply provided for, and that everything necessary for the comfort of the sick and wounded is promptly supplied, it will be imperative upon you to keep a reserve store, at all times well stocked, and to insist upon the Surgeon-Major in charge of each hospital supplementing his stores regularly from your depôt.

49. All supplies sent out by you should be accompanied by a delivery note and an invoice of the articles.

50. You are authorized, when necessary, to make purchases of medical comforts and other stores, when supplies are not obtainable in the proper way from this Department. The necessity for such purchases should be certified to by the Deputy Surgeon-General or by the Major-General Commanding.

51. You will issue medical comforts and other stores on requisition of the regimental or other medical officer in charge of hospitals, such requisitions to be countersigned by the Deputy Surgeon-General or principal Medical Officer.

52. When sick or wounded are sent home, or from one station to another, in ordinary hired transport, you will provide, on the requisition of the Hospital Surgeon, countersigned by the Deputy Surgeon-General, or principal officer in charge, such medical comforts and hospital stores as may be so ordered.

53. A hospital car, with dispensary kitchen, and accommodation for a Surgeon and three assistants, will be placed at the disposal of this Department by the Canadian Pacific Railway Co., for the transport of the sick and wounded between points furthest west and Winnipeg, and all such are to be transported if possible by that hospital car.

54. If you are in doubt as to the meaning of any of the above instructions, or should you require any further information upon any point, you will please, if the principal medical officer in charge be not at hand, to communicate directly with this Department.

55. I must ask you to be as economical in the use of the telegraph wire as possible, and to incur no expense of any kind for hospital stores unless upon requisition, as hereinbefore directed, duly signed or countersigned by the Deputy Surgeon-General, or principal medical officer in charge of the Troops in Manitoba and the North West.

I have the honor to be, Sir,
Your obedient servant,
D. BERGIN,
Medical Director-General.

(F).—REPORT OF SURGEON-MAJOR JAMES KERR,
WINNIPEG FIELD HOSPITAL.

WINNIPEG, April 16, 1886.

D. BERGIN, ESQ., M.P.,
  Ottawa.

SIR,

I have the honor herewith to submit to you a report of the Winnipeg Field Hospital during the time it was under my charge. To explain the date at which this report is sent in, I have to state that, until I received your telegram a few days ago, I was not aware that any report was required from me; I naturally supposed that the report would be furnished by my successor, Dr. Codd, when the Hospital was closed. I was placed in charge of sick volunteers by the Deputy Surgeon-General, Dr. Roddick, on Apl. 14th, 1885, and I immediately proceeded to make arrangements for their hospital accommodation, which was, with the concurrence of the D. S G., agreed with the directors of the Winnipeg General Hospital, to place the sick volunteers in a portion of their building to be specially set apart for that purpose. It was so decided, in consideration of this plan being much more consistent with affording the militia invalids the best care and treatment during their sickness, and, at the rate agreed, entailing a very much less expenditure than the renting and equipment of a building here. I refer specially to this arrangement, as during the first few weeks that I had charge of the Militia Hospital within the General Hospital serious annoyance and embarrassment to the proper discharge of my duties was offered by the arrival of other Surgeons, who represented themselves as authorized either to supersede myself and assistants in our positions, or to establish another hospital, and close up the one that had been thus organized.

By the enclosed list, you will find the numbers treated in the Hospital from 13th April to 15th August, while I had charge of this Hospital.

The majority of the cases during the first month were colds and other affections incurred owing to the exposure and fatigue during that part of the journey where the soldiers were marched over the uncompleted part of the Canadian Pacific Railway north of Lake Superior.

During my service, there was furnished a daily sick report to the Brigade Office here, also discharge and admission sheet of all cases admitted and discharged, with weekly statement of dietaries and hospital comforts supplied; besides a weekly report was furnished the D. S. G., and as soon as the request was made, a daily report was also furnished your office at Ottawa. In addition, I had histories written of each case during its stay in Hospital, before any history books were supplied; these were afterwards copied into the history books supplied from Ottawa. I am sorry that I cannot return a complete set of histories; they have been deprived of their covers, and a large number are missing. All the papers and forms in my possession were handed over by me to Dr. King, who was then acting as House Surgeon. There were appointed with me an Assistant Surgeon and three Dressers; the entire number treated in the hospital during the four months it was under my care was 81, leaving 10 in hospital. The death-rate will be seen by the enclosed tables to be very low. No complaints of want of proper care or feeding came under my notice.

I must mention that the comfort of the military invalids was materially increased by frequent and liberal donations of fruit, flowers, reading matter and invalid chairs by the ladies of Winnipeg.

The operations performed in the Hospital included incision in a case of emphysema, with drainage and antiseptic dressings. (Harrison, 91st.)

Excision of a large hydrocele of the neck, situated deeply at base of the neck, in contact with carotid sheath and subclavian artery. (Kilburne, 91st.)

Incision of knee-joint and extraction of bullet. (Eggett, Montreal Garrison Artillery.)

These constitute the major operations—they all ran an aseptic course, and resulted in complete cures. The minor surgical operations consisted in incision and drainage of abscess, making center openings for cure of purulent accumulations and sinuses.

Extraction of a bullet from a sinus in the case, and removal of necrosed fragment of bone from bullet tracks.

My duties, in addition to daily attendance on the Hospital, also included those of Acting Brigade-Surgeon at Winnipeg, daily attendance at the Brigade Office, and attending to the requirements of the various corps on their way to the front, and the other duties connected with this district, as a base of supplies.

I must apologize for the imperfect character of this report. Had I been asked for it I could necessarily have made it much fuller, when I had possession of all the papers connected with this Hospital, as a Base Hospital, and with all the facts fresh in my mind, but I must emphatically assert that your telegram was the first intimation I had of a report being requested of me.

I have the honor to be, Sir,

Your obedient servant,

JAMES KERR,

Late Surgeon-Major, Winnipeg Field Hospital.

NAME.	REGIMENT.	ADMITTED.	DISCHARGED.	DISEASE OR INJURY.	RESULT.
J. Greene	91st.	5.4.85	30.5.85	Typhoid.	Cured.
P. Peterson	91st.	6.4.85	4.5.85	Rheumatism.	"
U. Lortie	9th.	12.4.85	22.4.85	Cellulitis.	"
J. Hewitt	12th.	12.4.85	16.4.85	Bronchitis.	"
A. Deguise	9th.	13.4.85	17.4.85	Tonsillitis.	"
A. Blais	9th.	13.4.85	30.4.85	"	Died.
A. Boucher	9th.	13.4.85	16.4.85	Hemorrhoids.	Cured.
T. H. Trudel	9th.	13.4.85	17.4.85	Hemorrhoids.	"
A. Bastien	9th.	13.4.85	16.5.85	Pleurisy.	"
A. Campbell	91st.	13.4.85	4.5.85	Typhoid.	"
S. Rogers	Q. O. R.	13.4.85	14.5.85	Pneumonia.	"

Ten remaining in Hospital after 15th August.

These patients were in Hospital on 14th April.

John Harrison	91st.	22.5.85	......	Emphyzema.	
Geo. McIntosh	W. L. I.	25.5.85	31.7.85	Optic Neuritis.	Cured.
R. Eggett	M. G. A.	3.6.85	8.7.85	Gunshot wound of knee	"
H. Corbett, M.D.	Field Hospital.	4.6.85	29.6.85	Cirrhosis of liver.	Died.
F. Heany	10th Royals.	9.6.85	18.6.85	Erysipelas.	Cured.
C. S. Strong	Midland.	11.6.85	15.6.85	Alcoholism.	"
C. S. Strong	Midland.	23.6.85	26.6.85	Alcoholism.	"
John Hayton	M. G. A.	25.6.85	4.7.85	Rheumatism.	"
C. E. Kemp	90th.	27.6.85	......	Bullet-w'd of abdomen.	
J. W. Bruce	91st.	11.7.85	......	Injury to knee joint.	
Thos. Fisk	Steel's Scouts.	13.7.85	......	Bullet-wound of arm.	

Name.	Regiment.	Admitted.	Discharged.	Disease or Injury.	Result.
Thos. Reynolds	"B" Battery.	13.7.85	16.7.85	Com. fract. of humerus	Cured.
J. Marcotte	65th.	13.7.85	19.7.85	" " of clavicle.	"
W. J. Cantwell	10th Royals.	15.7.85	19.7.85	Wound of thigh.	"
Henry Wilson	10th "	15.7.85	......	Wound of lung.	
A. S. Martin	10th "	15.7.85	19.7.85	Bullet-w'd of shoulder.	
James Eager	10th "	15.7.85	19.7.85	Fracture of jaw.	
Samuel Bell	Midland.	15.7.85	21.7.85	Concussion of brain.	
Wm. Barton	Midland.	15.7.85	30.7.85	W'd. of thigh scrotum.	Cured.
S. M. Daly	Midland.	15.7.85	......	B.-wound of hand.	
F. J. Thompson	Boulton's Scouts.	15.7.85	......	Rheumatism.	
Hope Hay	Boulton's Scouts.	15.7.85	31.7.85	B.-wound of arm.	Cured.
W. Fairbanks	"A" Battery.	15.7.85	30.7.85	B.-wound of thigh.	"
Thos. Stout	"A" Battery.	15.7.85	21.7.85	Fracture of ribs.	"
James Dowker	10th.	15.7.85	11.8.85	Wound of thigh.	"
James McDonald		15.7.85	27.7.85	Pott's disease of spine.	
John McClintock	7th.	15.7.85	19.7.85	Rheumatism.	
John Warren	Q. O. R.	15.7.85	13.8.85	Pleurisy.	Cured.
J. F. Garden	Survey Corps.	15.7.85	30.7.85	B.-wound of shoulder.	Cured.
A. Doucet	Staff.	15.7.85	......	Bullet-wound of arm.	
R. S. Cook	French's Scouts.	15.7.85	......	Bullet-wound of leg.	
F. Bacon	G. G. B. G.	18.7.85	31.7.85	Bruise of abdomen.	
— Peters	7th.	18.7.85	21.7.85	Periostitis of arm.	
H. Heigham	Staff.	25.4.85	15.5.85	Pleurisy.	
Marshall Weir	Midland.	14.4.85	16.5.85	Exhaustion.	Cured.
John Smart	65th.	15.4.85	16.5.85	Rheumatism.	Sent Home.
Wm. Hurst	G. G. B. G.	15.4.85	21.4.85	Conjunctivitis.	Cured.
Fred. Cardew	W. L. I.	15.4.85	14.5.85	Scarlet fever.	"
James Nelson	G. G. B. G.	15.4.85	4.5.85	Wound of leg.	"
P. R. Beaumont	Q. O. R.	15.4.85	16.4.85	Pneumonia.	"
Alfred Laurencelle	9th.	15.4.85	18.4.85	Bronchitis.	"
Arthur Potvin	9th.	16.4.85	18.4.85	Diarrhœa.	"
David McKay	G. G. B. G.	16.4.85	20.4.85	Abscess of leg.	"
E. J. Murphy	G. G. B. G.	16.4.85	24.4.85	Wound of arm.	"
John Davidson	7th.	16.4.85	21.7.85	Typhoid fever.	"
Renne Miller	9th.	17.4.85	18.4.85	Wound of lip.	"
Wm. Land	7th.	17.4.85	21.7.85	Rheumatism.	"
Joseph Germain	9th.	19.4.85	22.4.85	Bronchitis.	"
J. T. Brennan	9th.	20.4.85	22.4.85	Dyspepsia.	"
J. B. Fortin	9th.	20.4.85	27.4.85	Bronchitis.	"
Peter Pouliot	9th.	20.4.85	22.4.85	Bronchitis.	"
Prospère Jobin	9th.	20.4.85	4.5.85	Tonsillitis.	"
Lucien Miller	9th.	20.4.85	16.5.85	Otitis Med. Cat.	"
W. L. Bruce	W. L. I.	21.4.85	8.6.85	Fract. of 1st Metacarpal.	"
L. J. Mylins	63rd.	23.4.85	27.4.85	Tonsillitis.	"
Thos. Menagh	G. G. B. G.	23.4.85	11.5.85	Debility.	"
Alfred Kilburn	91st.	25.4.85	18.6.85	Cyst of neck.	"
John Lanigan	Halifax Battery.	25.4.85	4.5.85	Eczema.	"
James Godwin	Midland Battery.	26.4.85	4.5.85	Bronchitis.	"
James Anderson	Midland Battery.	27.4.85	30.4.85	Debility.	"
Wilmot Lewis	Halifax Battery.	28.4.85	4.5.86	Tonsillitis.	"
H. Carroll	Halifax Battery.	28.4.85	18.5.85	Diarrhœa.	"
John Smart	65th.	1.5.85	16.5.85	Rheumatism.	"
Felix Heany	10th Royals.	5.5.85	13.5.85	Pleuro-pneumonia.	"
M. Stewart	12th.	14.5.85	18.5.85	Adenitis.	"
Wm. Shannon	12th.	14.5.85	5.6.85	Abscess.	"
Theo. Schwoenzer	35th.	14.5.85	18.5.85	Rheumatism.	"
Wm. Challacombe	M. G. A.	21.5.85	9.6.85	Simple fever, continued	"
Lewis Stead	10th Royals.	22.5.85	25.5.85	Bullet-wound of arm.	"

(D).—REPORT OF DEPUTY SURGEON-GENERAL.

MONTREAL, May 10th, 1886.

To D. BERGIN, ESQ, M.P.,
    Surgeon-General, Militia.

SIR,

In compliance with your instructions, I have the honor to submit the following report of the operations of the Medical Department of the North-West Field Force during the recent campaign.*

Having, on your recommendation, received from the Honorable Minister of Militia and Defence the appointment of Deputy Surgeon-General, I left Ottawa on the evening of April 7th, 1885, with orders to report to Major-General Middleton, who had by this time reached Troy, North-West Territories, with a portion of his command.

A Field Hospital Corps, which had already been organized by yourself, also accompanied me.

This was composed of the following members, drafted chiefly from the profession and medical schools of Montreal and Toronto :—

FIELD HOSPITAL CORPS No, 1.

Surgeon Major.—C. M. Douglas, V.C............Lakefield, Ont.
Surgeons.—James Bell........................Montreal, P.Q.
      E. A. Graveley....................Cornwall, Ont.
      W. R. Tracey.....................Belleville, "
      F. H. Powell.....................Ottawa, "
      W. W. Doherty....................Kingston, N.B.
      R. Reddick.......................West Winchester, Ont.
Dressers.—Alex. Kennedy, M.D ....Kingston, Ont.
      E. E. King, M.D..................Toronto, "
      J. S. Freebourne, M.D............Invermay,
      H. A. Wright, M.D................Qu'Appelle, N.W.T.
      A. N. Worthington................Sherbrooke, P.Q.
      J. A. Kinloch....................Montreal, P.Q.
      A. D. Stewart....................Arundel, P.Q.
      W. B. A. Hill....................Ottawa, Ont.
      W. P. Caven......................Toronto, "
      John Caven......................." "
      Thos. McKenzie...................Galt, "
      H. L. McInnes....................Winnipeg, Man.
      W. A. B. Hutton.................." "
      J. R. McIntyre..................." "
      G. H. Wilson....................." "
      W. R. Pringle....................Cornwall, Ont.
      W. J. Bradley....................Ottawa, "
      A. J. McDonell...................Morrisburg, Ont.
Orderlies.—D. Alma Macpherson.............Ottawa, Ont.
      J. Lawson........................" "
      J. Foran........................." "
      Henry Filteau....................Montreal, P. Q.
      H. H. Arrowsmith................." "

---

* This must of necessity be incomplete, owing to the fact that I was late in reaching the field of operations (the battle of Fish Creek having been fought before I arrived at the front), and, besides, many of the Regimental Surgeons have not favored me with reports.

We reached Winnipeg, via Chicago, on the morning of Sunday, 12th April.

I reported, as soon as possible, to Col. Jackson, who was doing duty as Deputy-Adjutant General. He kindly assisted me in billeting the Corps, and gave other advice and assistance, for which I feel deeply indebted.

I also telegraphed to Major-General Middleton, who at that time was somewhere between Touchwood Hills and Humboldt. My telegram was to the effect that I was anxious to furnish his Column with a Field Hospital outfit, and also to know his views regarding the location of a Base Hospital. He replied on the following day, ordering me to go to Swift Current and establish Base Hospital there, and reach him by the Saskatchewan, as the Fort Qu'Appelle route was likely to be impassable for a time, and was, in fact, about to be abandoned.

On the 13th, Dr. Sullivan, Purveyor-General, arrived in Winnipeg, in charge of medical and surgical outfit which had been shipped from Montreal. This latter consisted of instruments, drugs, appliances, necessaries, cots, mattrasses, stretchers, etc., arranged in four (4) complete sets for Field Hospital purposes.

Arrangements were made with the authorities of the Winnipeg General Hospital, for the accommodation of sick and wounded soldiers, the rate per diem being one dollar fifty cents ($1.50). I appointed Drs. Kerr and Mewburn to take charge of the wards set apart for the accommodation of the Troops.

Four students of the Winnipeg School of Medicine were added to the strength of the Corps.

Supt. Egan, of the Canadian Pacific Railway, kindly gave every assistance in procuring and fitting up a caboose and emigrant sleeper, to be subsequently used for purposes of transport. A box car was also secured for baggage and equipment.

I may say, in this connection, that the emigrant sleeper is especially adapted for the transportation of sick and wounded men, being arranged with berths similar to the ordinary Pullman car, but, with this great advantage for hospital purposes, viz., the entire absence of upholstery of any kind. It is also fitted with wash room and closet and heated with steam. With a very little trouble and expense the emigrant sleeper could be converted into a most admirable hospital car.

While in Winnipeg, I made inquiries regarding the equipment of the various Regimental Surgeons then serving with their corps in various parts of the Territories, and was surprised to learn that, without an exception, they were all very scantily provided with the medicines, instruments and dressings necessary for the campaign; in fact, I felt that, in the event of an epidemic or an engagement, it would be impossible for them to render the men that service which would be required.

On the 15th, I left Winnipeg for Swift Current, with the entire Corps.

On the advice of Lt.-Col. Van Straubenzie, who had joined our party on his way to the front via Qu'Appelle, and being most anxious to furnish the Surgeons in the Field with a more complete outfit, I again telegraphed Major General Middleton, suggesting that I might send a Surgeon and Dressers with a small hospital outfit by the Qu'Appelle route going on myself to Swift Current, as he had ordered. He promptly replied to the same effect as before, namely, that every thing should be sent by the River.

Major-General Laurie joined us at Troy, on his way from the front to Swift Current, to take charge of the base and line of communication. He also reported the trail to be in places almost impassable, thus bearing out the statement of the General.

Having ascertained that a detachment of the 35th regiment, encamped at Troy was in need of surgical aid, I left Surgeon Graveley and Assistant-Surgeon King to take charge until some other arrangement would be made.

On the afternoon of the 16th April, we reached Swift Current, the ground, covered with snow, and thermometer several degrees below freezing. Within sight of the railway were several " teepees " of Indians and Half-breeds. The Midland Battalion, under Lieut. Col. Williams, had arrived a short time before, and encamped near the railway station, awaiting further orders.

The Caboose, Emigrant sleeping car and baggage car were placed on a convenient siding, and occupied by Surgeons and Dressers, there being no house available, and no tents to spare.

April 17.—Five men belonging to Col. Otter's column were brought in, being invalided back during the day, from the Saskatchewan Landing and Battleford Trail.

Private Wiggins .... G. G. Foot Guards.
Sergeant Hewgill .... Q. O. R.
Private Bain .... Q. O. R.
" Birchall .... Q. O. R.
" Noudel .... Infantry School.

They were suffering mostly from cold and exposure, Pte. Wiggins having pneumonia. These were promptly billeted in a room adjoining the railway station.

April 19.—Surgeon-Major Douglas was ordered to report to Major-General Strange at Calgary, taking with him a full hospital outfit, and the following members of the corps :—

Surgeons.—W. R. Tracy,   F. H. Powell,
Dressers.—John Caven,   A. J. McDonell,
W. P. Caven,   W. B. A. Hill.
T. McKenzie,
Orderlies.—D. A. Macpherson, H. H. Arrowsmith.
J. Lawson,

Surgeon Reddick was ordered to Saskatchewan Landing to become permanently attached to the Midland Battalion, two companies of which were stationed at that place.

Assistant Surgeon Might, of the Midland Battalion, having become very much enfeebled from the journey, was ordered back to Qu'Appelle to relieve Surgeon Graveley, who, with Assistant-Surgeon King, came on at once to join the Field Hospital Corps.

April 21.—The "Red Cross" Corps, under Surgeon Nattrass, arrived this morning, and received orders to join Otter's column, then three days distant on the Battleford trail.

This Corps consisting of a Surgeon, Assistant Surgeon and eight Dressers, was organized in Toronto, and handsomely equipped by the citizens of that city. It promised to be a most efficient and useful body of men.

On the 22nd, Surgeon Bell of the Field Hospital Corps, left Swift Current with a complete Hospital outfit, and the following Surgeons and Dressers :—

Surgeons.—E. N. Graveley,   E. E. King.
Assistant Surgeons.—H. A. Wright,   J. S. Freebourne.
Dressers.—A. N. Worthington,   W. J. Bradley,
J. A. Kinloch,   H. L. McInnes,
W. R. Pringle,   W. A. B. Hutton.
Orderly.—J. Foran,

His orders were to take passage per Str. " Northcote," then lying at Saskatch-ewan Landing, her destination being some point on the river Saskatchewan nearest the headquarters in the field of Major-General Middleton. Lieut.-Col. Van Strau-benzie and Lieut.-Col. Williams, with four companies of his regiment, were also under orders to take passage by her.

This landing is the nearest point on the Saskatchewan River to Swift Current Station, being over thirty miles distant, and in the line of the Battleford Trail.

April 23rd, sick doing well, with the exception of Pte. Wiggins, whose symptoms are somewhat unfavorable, the inflammation having extended to the other lung.

The Steamer " Northcote " left Saskatchewan Landing.

April 24th, telegram from Major-General Middleton, giving a short account of Fish Creek Battle.

Owing to some delay in the transportation of the " Red Cross " Corps, and the urgent call for assistance and medical supplies from Brigade-Surgeon Strange of Otter's column, I dispatched Assistant Surgeons Kennedy and Doherty, and Dressers Wilson, McIntyre, Campbell and Hillier, with orders to overtake the column, if possible, before reaching Battleford.

Field Hospital Corps No. 2, in charge of Surgeon-Major Casgrain, arrived to-day.

The Surgeons, Dressers and Orderlies composing his corps were as follows :—

```
Surgeons.—N. O. Walker. ...................... Toronto, Ont.
           E. Hooper........................... Kingston,  "
           Francis Murray..................... Montreal, P.Q.
           E. Pelletier....................... Quebec,    "
           E. O. Cloutier..................... St. Arsene, "
Dressers.—W. J. McCuaig...................... Vankleek Hill, Ont.
           A. R. Turnbull..................... Duncanville,  "
           J. M. McKay........................ River John, N.B.
           J. F. Williams..................... Barrie, Ont.
           Fred. J. White..................... Shediac, N.B.
           A. J. Schmidt...................... Faribault, Minn.
           E. R. Bishop....................... Brantford, Ont.
           W. F. Graham....................... Bells Corners, Ont.
           N. Aikins.......................... Binbrook,   "
           S. T. Bell......................... Alliston,   "
           T. J. McDonald.....................   "         "
           Fred. Winnett...................... London,     "
           J. M. Thompson..................... Strathroy,  "
           T. F. Campbell..................... Appin,      "
           R. Hillier......................... Toronto,    "
           A. E. Collins...................... St. Catharines, "
           J. Rea............................. Toronto,    "
           James Park......................... Newcastle, N.B.
Apothecary.—W. H. Wilbur...................... Dorchester, N.B.
Orderlies.—W. T. Lawless ..................... Hull, P.Q.
           Wm. Francke........................ Toronto, Ont.
Cook.—Peter Nugent............ .......... Kingston,  "
```

These were all quartered in the emigrant sleeper.

Dr. Nattrass returned to Swift Current, to obtain, if possible, other transport, but as nothing better was available, he proceeded to Battleford without further delay.

April 26th.—Surgeon-Major Douglas returned from Calgary, bringing with him Dresser W. B. A. Hill and Orderly D. A. Macpherson, having attached Surgeon Powell and two dressers to Major General Strange's Column, and established a small Hospital at Calgary under the charge of Surgeon Tracy. My original intention in sending Surgeon-Major Douglas to Calgary was to have him attached to Major General Strange's Column, but the Brigade Surgeon of that Column considered that his services would hardly be required, and besides it was found impossible to obtain transport for his equipment.

April 29th.—Anxiety regarding the position of Steamer "Northcote" was somewhat relieved by the arrival in camp of a scout who reported her grounded ten miles from the Elbow of the South Saskatchewan, and with very little prospect of her getting off.

The Field hospital outfit intended for General Middleton's Column being, in consequence, indefinitely delayed, and knowing how urgently certain articles would be required after the battle of Fish Creek, I determined to proceed to the front without delay via the Moose Jaw Trail. Surgeon-Major Casgrain detailed from his Field Hospital Corps to accompany me, Surgeon Pelletier and Dressers White, Schmidt, McDonald and Rea. A large field pannier and as much else in the shape of necessaries, dressing, stretchers, etc., as could be carried in an ordinary waggon were quickly got ready.

I proceeded the same evening by rail to Moosejaw, where by previous arrangement, Mr. James Ross was awaiting me with the waggons, etc., necessary for the journey.

The Moose Jaw trail had been abandoned for many months, owing to the hostile behavior of the Indians comprising White Cap's Band of the Moose Woods reserve, as well as from the unsettled state of that part of the country generally. From information obtained from surveyors and others, I was, however, convinced that it would be in good condition, and, in fact, at that time the only available route to the front. I venture to say that, had it been better known, it would at that time have been selected for purposes of transport in preference to the river route.

April 30.—Left Moose Jaw this afternoon, about two o'clock, with two double waggons, a cart for carrying fodder, and two spare horses, Mr. James Ross kindly consenting to act as guide. The same evening we reached the house of the last settler, some thirty miles from Moose Jaw, and put up for the night.

May 1.—Travelled hard all day, stopping only to feed horses, and reached the Elbow at 7.30 p. m. Here we found Capt. Dennis encamped with a detachment of the Intelligence Corps. (They had been ordered here to guard this exposed part of the river during the passage of the "Northcote" and also to stop Indian and Half-breed fugitives.)

Capt. Dennis reported the "Northcote" as having passed the Elbow the day before, and proceeded beyond the beat of his scouts, which would be at least twenty miles north of that point. We encamped here for the night.

May 2.—Started at 3 a. m. Late in the afternoon, we met Major Bedson on his way to find the "Northcote" with some fifty teams, the intention being to lighten her, so that she might be enabled better to cross the various sand bars which were constantly impeding her.

Heard from him that the wounded were being brought on to Saskatoon under charge of Brigade-Surgeon Orton.

May 3.—At two a. m. reached Saskatoon, having made the journey from Moose Jaw in the then unprecedented time of sixty hours.

News received of the battle of Cut Knife Hill.

Found that the wounded had just arrived from the front, under charge of Brigade-Surgeon Orton, assisted by Surgeon Ralston of Boulton's Scouts, Assistant-Surgeon Moore of the "90th" and Dr. Willoughby, a local physician. There were thirty-five (35) wounded in all, billeted on the inhabitants of the place and in the schoolhouse.

Surgeon-Major Douglas had arrived an hour or two before me, having performed the remarkable feat of paddling alone in a canoe from Saskatchewan Landing to this place, a distance of over two hundred miles. He overtook the "Northcote" some fifty miles up the river, passed her, and reached Saskatoon in less than five days. He was the first to bring tidings of the whereabouts of the "Northcote" from the time that she passed the Elbow. I consider that Surgeon-Major Douglas deserves due credit for his pluck and endurance.

During the day, Surgeon-Major Douglas took over the wounded from Brigade-Surgeon Orton, who, with Surgeon Ralston and Assistant-Surgeon Moore, returned immediately to the front by trail.

Surgeon Pelletier and the dressers who came with me were detailed for duty under Surgeon-Major Douglas.

The following is a complete list of the sick and wounded drafted back from Fish Creek :

Captain Wm. Clark, 90th Battalion.	Staff Sergeant Mawhinney, "A" Battery.
Private David Hislop, "	Driver Michael Wilson, "
Corporal Lethbridge, "	Trooper Charles King, Boulton's Mounted Inf'ty
" J. B. D. Code, "	" V. Bruce, " " "
Private W. W. Matthews, "	" Thomson, " " "
" M. O. R. Jarvis, "	" J. Langford, " " "
" C. H. Kemp, "	Herbert Perrin, " " "
" Wm. Wainwright, "	Captain M. Gardiner, " " "
" W. Restall, "	Private R. H. Dunn, "C" School of Infantry.
" Edward Lowell, "	" R. Jones, " " "
" A. S. Blackwood, "	" E. Harris, " " "
" G. W. C. Swan, "	" Harry Jones, " " "
" W. McRobie, "	" E. McDonald, " " "
" W. H. Canniff, "	Col.-Sergt. R. Cumming, " " "
Sergeant Hurrill, 90th Battalion.	Private J. Cane, 10th Royal Grenadiers.
Private E. Moisan, "A" Battery.	" J. Gray, " "
" W. Woodman, "A" Battery.	Cook P. J. Reggin, " "
" A. Imrie, "	Corp. J. Billinghurst, " "
" Asselin, "	Private Arch. McLean, "Midland" Battalion.
Bombardier D. Taylor, "	

May 4.—At daybreak, Major Bedson and myself went up the river some distance in search of the "Northcote," and found her stuck fast on a sand-bar, about five miles above Saskatoon. She soon afterwards reached Saskatoon, where Surgeon Bell with his Field Hospital Corps disembarked. After a short delay here, the steamer proceeded on her way to the Fish Creek camp, and I took passage in her for the purpose of reporting myself to the General, taking with me Dressers Pringle and Kinloch to be attached to the 90th Regiment and Boulton's Scouts respectively.

After many delays, caused by the grounding of the Steamer, the camp was reach at 7 o'clock next morning.

I was courteously received by the General, and discussed with him, and Brigade-Surgeon Orton, questions of Field and Base hospitals and Medical matters, referred to in your General Orders, which will be found in the Appendix.

It was decided to establish a Field Hospital at Saskatoon, and a Base Hospital at either Swift Current or Moose Jaw, depending on whether or not the river route remained available.

As another engagement was imminent within a few days, it was decided to make provision at Saskatoon for at least fifty more wounded.

The General ordered me to send on without delay the Field Hospital Corps, originally intended for his Column, under charge of Surgeon Bell.

I left the camp at 2 o'clock in the afternoon of the same day, taking with me in one of the ambulances Capt. Doucet, A.D.C., who had received a serious gunshot wound of the right elbow joint. Having to travel very slowly on his account, we did not reach Saskatoon till midnight,

May 5.—At the request of the General, I visited on the way back a man named McDonald, lying ill in a house about five miles from Fish Creek. He was suffering from "caries" of the spine. I ordered him to Saskatoon, as it was unsafe for him to be in such close proximity to the enemy's country.

May 6.—Surgeon Bell, with the following members of the Corps, viz :—

Surgeon.—Graveley.
Assistant Surgeons.—Wright,   Freebourne.
Dressers.—White,   Hutton,
          Bradley,   Worthington,
          McInnes,

left this morning to join General Middleton's Column, his instructions being to place himself under the orders of Brigade-Surgeon Orton.

Spent most of the day in examining the wounded and consulting regarding their condition with Surgeon-Major Douglas.

Telegraphed Dr. Kerr of Winnipeg to send Nurse Miller, of the Winnipe gGeneral Hospital, without delay to the Front, via Moose Jaw trail, other Nurses to follow as soon as selected.

May 7th.—Busy organizing. Appointed Dr. Willoughby to the position of Assistant-Purveyor, and Mr. James McGowan, a resident of Saskatoon, to that of Supply Officer.

Requisitioned the three largest houses in the place for hospitals, so as to concentrate the wounded, and thus lighten the work of attendance.

The village of Saskatoon is the chief settlement of the Temperance Colonization Company, situated on the east bank of the South Saskatchewan, about seventeen miles south of Clarke's Crossing, and twenty miles north of the Moose Woods Indian Reserve.

There are about twenty wooden dwellings and a commodious school house in the place. It is well situated from a sanitary standpoint, the banks of the river here being high, and the soil naturally porous and dry. In fact, it would be difficult to find a better "sanitarium," and I am convinced that much of the success which followed the treatment of the sick and wounded billeted here was due to the remarkably healthy condition of the place.

The buildings referred to, which I requisitioned, were especially well placed on the bank of the river, and, being unfinished, could be conveniently arranged for hospital purposes. When filled with the wounded, it was computed that every man had upwards of one thousand (1000) cubic feet of air space. This is, of course, a small proportion, but the ventilation was so thorough, and the air-supply so abundant and uncontaminated, that I considered it sufficient. The ventilation was simply by opposite windows and additional openings in the ceilings. Two of the buildings were two-storey, the other one-storied.

The strictest rules were laid down by General Orders with regard to the immediate removal of all excreta and foul dressings, and privies were constructed at convenient distances from the buildings. A man was detailed to apply dry earth frequently, so that the discharges were never left uncovered for longer than a few moments; water was abundantly supplied from the river for cleansing purposes, while delicious drinking water was obtained from a spring some two miles from the village.

The food was at first a little scanty; under the circumstances, no complaint could be made. There was an abundance of fresh meat, a large drove of cattle having, through the admirable foresight of the Commissariat Department, arrived simultaneously with the wounded. Beef tea was thus readily obtained, and milk also in fair amount. All the eggs, butter and flour available were purchased from the settlers, which, with the necessaries and comforts of the outfit which I brought from Moosejaw with me, served to make up a very fair dietary.

For the following few days, the members of the staff were constantly engaged attending to the wounded, as, owing to the absence of skilled women, much of the nursing had to be done by ourselves. Two or three of the farmers' wives of the place kindly rendered what assistance they could, but their time was chiefly occupied in the preparation of food.

The cases at this time requiring most attention were those of Capt. Clark, wounded through the back, not penetrating; Capt. Doucet, A.D.C.; Corp. Code, wounded through both legs; Pte. Lethbridge, penetrating wound of chest; Pte. Hislop, whose arm had been amputated near the shoulder; and Pte. Caniff, shot in, the elbow-joint.

May 12.—Nurse Miller arrived to-day, and immediately took charge of the wounded.

News received of Battle of Batoche, and complete rout of Riel and his followers.

Sent courier to General, asking him to relieve Surgeon Bell, as I would require him to take charge of the wounded as they came in from Batoche. Five men wounded in the early part of the fighting arrived from the front to-day, also the body of Private Hardisty.

Corporal Code much worse, having had an alarming hemorrhage from one of the wounds in the leg; very little hope of his recovery. Other serious cases improving.

Received orders from the General to prepare for the Batoche wounded.

May 14.—Steamer "Northcote" arrived with wounded, including two Half-breeds—Assistant-Surgeon Wright and Dresser Fred. White in charge. The bodies of Capt. French, Lieut. Fitch, Lieut. Kippen, and Pte. Fraser were also on board.

A violent rainstorm coming on, it was decided not to transfer the wounded to the Hospital until the following day.

May 15.—Private Watson died during the night on board the "Northcote." Corp. Code also die during the night.

Commenced early moving the wounded, dressing each case as he came into the Hospital. The following is a complete list of those who were drafted back from Batoche :

Sergeant F. R. Jakes,	90th Battalion.	Private Jas. Marshall, 10th Royal Grenadiers.
Corporal Wm. Kemp,	"	" A. Martin, " "
Private R. Barron,	"	" Jno. Quigley, " "
" Jos. Chambers,	"	" Alf. Scoville, " "
" Jas. Dowker,	"	" Lewis Stead, " "
" M. Erickson,	"	Drummer M. Ganghan, " "
" F. Alex. Watson,	"	Captain T. C. Lazier, "Midland " Battalion.
" A. L. Young,	"	Lieutenant J. E. Halliwell, "
Gunner N. Charpentier, "A" Battery.		" Geo. Laidlaw, "
" W. Fairbanks,	"	Color-Sergt. W. Atkins, "
" M. Twohey,	"	" W. T. Wrighton, "
Driver T. J. Stout,	"	Sergeant A. E. Christie, "
Captain J. F. Manley, 10th Royal Grenadiers.		Corporal E. A. E. Halliwell, "
" Jas. Mason,	" "	Private W Barton, "
Corporal Jas. Foley,	" "	" Simcoe Daley, "
Private W. Cantwell,	" "	" W. Powell, "
" R. Cook,	" "	Lieutenant J. F. Garden, Intelligence Corps.
" Jas. Eager,	" "	Private R. S. Cooke, French's Scouts.
" H. Milson,	" "	

May 16th.—Surgeon Bell arrived from the front, and was immediately put in charge of the Hospital, with the rank of Surgeon-Major, in accordance with your orders. I append Dr. Bell's report of the Battle of Batoche.

SURGEON-MAJOR BELL'S REPORT OF BATOCHE.

T. G. RODDICK, ESQ.,
Deputy Surgeon-General, Saskatoon.

SIR,
In compliance with your instructions, I started from Saskatoon on the morning of May 6, with the following members of the corps :—

Surgeon.—E. A Gravely.
Assistant Surgeons.—H. A. Wright,   J. S. Freebourne.
Dressers.—White,   Hutton.
           Bradley,   Worthington.
           McInnes,

The Rev. D. M. Gordon, of Winnipeg, was also of the party.

We encamped that night at McIntosh, six miles from Fish Creek. Left the next morning at five o'clock, and were just in time to transfer our stores to the transport waggons, and to go on with the Column. We reached Gabriel Dumont's Landing that afternoon, and remained there for the night. Next morning we struck back from the river trail, and camped at Beautiful Spot, about eight miles north-east of Batoche.

Next morning, May 9th, we left camp at about six o'clock, going in with twenty empty waggons for the wounded, with a bale of hay in each, and our complete hospital equipment. Each man of the Ambulance Corps was equipped with a "haversack" in which he carried iodoform, bandages, and some absorbent cotton, and two of them had Esmarch's rubber bands. We reached Batoche after the fighting began, about half-past eight o'clock. We first located our hospital waggons in a ravine, near the church at Batoche, but subsequently took possession of the church, and had the wounded brought in there to be treated. We had the assistance of two or three nuns, with blankets and utensils, while we remained in the church.

About two o'clock in the afternoon, we were ordered to leave the church, and, putting the wounded into waggons, retired some little distance. For the remainder of the afternoon, we were at some considerable uncertainty as to our future movements.

Finally, late in the evening, when an entrenched camp was decided on and located, we pitched the hospital tent at the edge of a slough in the centre. This was the only tent pitched at Batoche, until after the conclusion of the fight, when two additional bell tents were pitched to accommodate the wounded. We spread hay on the soft wet ground at the edge of the slough on which our tent was situated, and laid the wounded on stretchers in the tent.

Several bullets went through the tent that evening, and on subsequent occasions; but, owing to the dip of the ground, the wounded men were out of range, the bullets passing through the tent three or four feet from the ground.

The first man wounded was Gunner Charpentier of " A " Battery, a Winchester bullet passing through the left calf and into the right knee-joint, shattering the joint, and penetrating the calf muscles.

Driver Stout, of " A " Battery, was run over by a nine-pound gun, early in the morning.

Phillips, of " A " Battery, shot in the ravine, was dead when recovered.

Private Moore of 10th Royal Grenadiers was struck in the right parietal eminence by a spent bullet late in the evening, causing compound fracture of the skull. We had decided to trephine the skull, but before it could be done he had died.

Captain Mason, 10th Royal Grenadiers, was also shot early in the morning of the first day, bullet striking him in the left lumbar region, and passing deeply through the muscles, making its exit near the anterior superior illiac crest.

Altogether, the casualties of the first day were two killed and nine wounded.

The casualties of the next two days were slight, but on the evening of the charge we had our hands full.

Altogether, there were eight men killed and forty-five wounded at Batoche. Some of the latter were so slightly wounded that they were not sent back to Saskatoon.

Private Watson died on board the " Northcote " before reaching Saskatoon.

On the 13th of May, the steamer " Northcote " was got ready, and as fast as possible the wounded men were transferred in waggons to the ferry, which was about one and a half miles distant from our camp. By four o'clock in the afternoon, all the wounded were comfortably stowed away on board the boat, and she left for Saskatoon.

Dr. Wright and Mr. White took charge of them on the trip to Saskatoon.

I also sent Jobin and Delorme, two of the Rebel Council, who had been picked up on the field previously, seriously wounded. Three of them had been brought to our camp badly wounded, and died in the meantime.

I beg to attach herewith a report of the operations performed at Batoche.

I have the honor to be, Sir,

Your obedient servant,

JAMES BELL,
Surgeon-Major.

―――――

REPORT OF OPERATIONS PERFORMED ON THE FIELD, AT BATTLE OF BATOCHE, MAY 9TH TO 13TH, 1885.

Lieut. Garden, Intelligence Corps.—I extracted the bullet, and a good deal of cloth, from the outside of the arm, on the morning of the charge, May 13.

Gunner Fairbanks, "A" Battery.—Bullet extracted from leg.

Private Eager, 10th Royal Grenadiers.—Shot through lower jaw. Fragments of the shattered bone were removed on the night of May 12th, by Dr. Orton and myself. He lost a great deal of blood, as there was some difficulty in ligaturing the vessels.

Private Martin, 10th Royal Grenadiers.—Bullet extracted from inner angle scapula by Dr. Ryerson, on Sunday, 10th May.

R. S. Cooke, French's Scouts.—Compound fracture of the head of tibia. Leg was put in blue clay splint by Drs. Orton and Codd, on Sunday morning, May 10th. He was wounded on first day.

Corporal Kemp, 90th Battalion.—Bullet extracted from temple immediately in front of the ear, having broken the bridge of the nose, and passed through eyeball.

Lieut. Halliwell, "Midland Battalion."—Dr. Horsey and myself removed a bullet from his left shoulder, where it was lodged in the capsule of the joint, having shattered the coracoid process, and carried away anterior surface of clavicle, being a round bullet.

Private Barton, "Midland Battalion."—The right testicle was carried out of the scrotum, a Winchester bullet passing completely through it. The diseased tissue was pared away, and the testicle returned to the scrotum, having been cleansed with carbolic lotion and the scrotum brought together with sutures, leaving capillary drainage.

Private A. L. Young, 90th Battalion.—Bullet removed from lower third of thigh, posterior side, by Dr. Whiteford and myself.

Private H. Milson, 10th Grenadiers.—Bullet was removed from beneath the skin on the antero-lateral portion of left chest, having entered between the spines of the vertebræ on the right side.

The cots which had been supplied were found somewhat defective in both construction and quality of material, so that the bulk of them were discarded entirely, and wooden cots substituted for them. Fortunately, there was no scarcity of mattrasses, so that the beds could be made very comfortable.

The 7th Battalion, under Col. Williams, arrived about this time from Saskatchewan Landing, en route for Clarke's Crossing, and left us a liberal supply of bacon, sugar, candles, etc.

May 19.—Steamer "Northcote" arrived to-day from the front, bringing Capt. Young and Guard in charge of the prisoner, Louis Riel. Capt. Young disembarked at Saskatoon, preferring to take the trail for Moosejaw, on his way to Regina. To strengthen the guard, I sent four convalescents with the party. The Captain of the "Northcote" had orders from the General to place the steamer at my disposal, for the transport of convalescents to the "Elbow," whence they were to take the trail to Moosejaw. Twenty-eight men, in charge of Surgeon Major Douglas and Surgeon Walker, who arrived from the Base the day before, accordingly embarked on the 20th May.

The "Northcote," being a large and commodious steamer, was well adapted for purposes of transport. The men were made very comfortable in the spacious staterooms and saloon.

Meanwhile, at the Base, important changes were taking place. Major-General Laurie and staff, and Purveyor-General Sullivan and staff, had within a few days moved their headquarters from Swift Current to Moosejaw, the intention being to utilize the Moosejaw trail, as the chief line of communication with the front. The " Moose Hotel," a conveniently constructed building, had been requisitioned for hospital purposes by the Purveyor-General, and expeditiously put in order so as to accommodate about thirty patients, with medical attendants and nurses.

May 23.—Two Nurses, an assistant and a helper, arrived to-day by trail and were at once put on duty under the superintendence of Nurse Miller. The latter had hitherto been most indefatigable in her attendance on the wounded. In fact, much of the success which attended the treatment of our wounded at Saskatoon was undoubtedly due to the skill, kindness and untiring devotion of Nurse Miller. Nurses Elking and Hamilton are likewise deserving of praise for their unremitting attention to duty.

May 25.—Being anxious to inspect the Base Hospital at Moosejaw, I started early this morning by trail, reaching the Elbow the same night. I here learned that the " Northcote " had reached her destination and landed the wounded the day previous, returning immediately down the river.

I accomplished the journey to Moosejaw in forty-eight hours. The trail had been very much improved since my journey north. Lieut.-Governor Dewdney having ordered the bridges to be repaired, etc. But, notwithstanding this, in some places it had become very rough, owing to the heavy transport which had recently passed over it. There is one serious objection to this trail, namely, the scarcity of water, but this could readily be overcome by sinking wells at reasonable distances.

The following report of the journey of the convalescent wounded from Saskatoon was handed me by Surgeon-Major Douglas :

Moosejaw, May 26th, 1885

To Dr. Surgeon-General Roddick,

Moosejaw.

Sir,

I have the honor to report my arrival at this place in charge of a party of wounded invalids from the Field Hospital, Saskatoon.

LIST OF INVALIDS PROCEEDING FROM SASKATOON TO MOOSEJAW.

10th Royal Grenadiers.
1. Master Cook, P. J. Reggin, rheumatism.
2. Private J. Bellinghurst, "
3. " J. Cane, G. S. wound hand (R).
4. " A. Scovell, " arm (R.)
5. " Wainwright, rheumatism.
6. Bugler Goughal, G. S. wound of hand.*

90th Regiment.
7. Private Erikson, G. S. wound shoulder (L).
8. " R. Barrow, " hand (L).
9. " Blackwood, " nates (L).
10. " Jarvis, " forearm (R).
11. " Restale, rheumatism.

A Battery.
12. Staff Sergt. MacWhinney, G. S. wound, R. arm and thumb.
13. Bomb'r. Taylor, G. S. wound R. thigh.
14. Gunner Irwin, " "
15. " Woodman, " shoulder (R).

16. Gunner Asselin, G. S. wound shoulder (L).
17. " E. Moisan, " abdomen.
18. " Twohy, " thigh (L).
19. Driver Wilson, amputation of left arm.
C School.
20. C Sergt. Cummings, G. S. wound thigh (R).
21. Private Dunn, excision right elbow.
22. " Harris, G.S. wound right arm.
23. " Matthews, " "
24. " H. Jones, " face.
25. " R. Jones, " elbow (R).
Midland Battalion.
26. " G. Smith, scald of leg.
Boulton's Mounted Infantry.
27. Trooper Perrn. amputation of arm.
28. " McNiell, syphilis.

*10th Royal Grenadiers (Omitted.)
29. Private Robt. Cook, G. S. wound right arm.

We left Saskatoon early on the morning of the 21st inst., having embarked on board steamer " Northcote, " on the previous evening. The voyage up the river on board of this steamer was most satisfactory. The wounded, nearly all of whom were comparatively slight cases and convalescent, were well accommodated in cabins, state-rooms or on mattrasses on the cabin floor for the night, and there were facilities for dressing those cases that required it in the wash-room. On the 23rd we arrived at the "Elbow " of the South Saskatchewan river, and continued our journey to Moosejaw overland, next morning, nine teams having been procured for our conveyance. The journey over the trail was more trying to some of the severer cases of wounds, especially to one of compound fracture of the forearm and to a case of amputation of the arm. A tent was procured for the seven cases at the Elbow, and another was found about two-thirds of the way from the river, so that on the second night out all could be accommodated. We arrived about 10 a. m. to-day, the distance from the Elbow, 50 miles, having been performed in two days, five hours.

The invalids were at once taken to the Hospital at Moosejaw, where ample provision had been made for them.

I would suggest that no serious cases of wounds should be sent by this route, the journey overland in unsuitable vehicles being too trying. Fortunately, there are only a few cases of this kind at Saskatoon ; and when the Hospital is broken up, then they could be sent direct to Winnipeg by the Hudson Bay Co.'s boats as soon as the navigation of Lake Winnipeg can be preformed by them.

I have the honor to be, Sir,
Your obedient servant,
C. M. DOUGLAS,
In charge of Field Hospital.

May 27.—Accompanied by Major-General Laurie, Purveyor-General Sullivan, and Surgeon-Major Casgrain, I inspected the new Base Hospital. It consisted of a long, narrow, wooden building, two storied, the ground floor being conveniently partitioned off, having in front an office, a portion of which was now used by the Apothecary. Within this was a wide hallway of sufficient capacity for five beds. Further on was a large, square, well ventilated room, in which ten beds were placed; ample air being afforded. Behind this again a spacious kitchen, with cupboards adjoining.

The upper story was divided up into small rooms, some of which were large enough for two patients. A recreation tent, cookshop and marquee for convalescents were being erected on the large green adjoining the Hospital. Privies and cesspools were erected at a convenient distance.

Surgeon-Major Casgrain was ordered to take charge of the Base Hospital, his staff consisting of:—Surgeon Walker ; Dressers Collins, Thompson, McCuaig, Turnbull, McKay, Bishop, Graham, Aikins, Park ; Orderlies Lawless and Francke; Apothecary Wilbur.

May 28.—At my suggestion, Major-General Laurie appointed an invaliding Board, composed of Surgeon-Major Douglas, Surgeon-Major Casgrain and myself. We examined ten men whom we considered to be sufficiently convalescent to undertake the journey home. I also discharged from duty Dressers White, McKay, Thompson, Turnbull, Collins, McCuaig and Lawless, as there was not likely to be any more necessity for their services.

May 30.—The Nurses arranged for and sent by you from Toronto, namely, four Sisters of St. John the Divine and three skilled Nurses, arrived this morning, in charge of Dr. Caniff. Their arrival was most opportune, as some of the men were much in need of skilled nursing

Arrangements were made for Sisters and Nurses to reside in a building adjoining the Hospital. The Lady Superior at once took charge, so that in a short time, things were put into good shape.

June 1.—Went to Qu'Appelle station, and inspected the small Hospital in charge of Dr. O. C. Edwards. This is a small building, having three wards, which, in the early part of the campaign, was filled with men drafted back from General Middleton's Column, but now containing only one patient. This was the late Dr. James Corbett, who took ill with dropsy on his way to report to me, and was never well enough to proceed further. He was being well cared for, and was improving, but, as I was about to close the Hospital, I ordered him back to the Winnipeg Hospital, where he was subsequently treated as a private patient up to the time of his death.

June 3rd.—Returned from Qu'Appelle again, inspected Hospital, and had reason to compliment the Lady Superior on the efficiency of her staff and the admirable condition of the Hospital generally.

June 5th.—Received a telegram from the Minister to the effect that Dr. Boyd, sent by the Princess Louise with a medical and surgical outfit, and large fund for distribution, was on his way to Winnipeg and would expect me to take him in charge.

I at once proceeded to Winnipeg, received Dr. Boyd on his arrival, and, on the 8th, left with him for Moosejaw, to give him an opportunity of seeing the Base Hospital.

He expressed himself as highly pleased with the arrangements, and compared our work most favorably with what he had already seen in recent campaigns in Servia, Zululand, etc.

I spent the next three or four days in Moosejaw, assisting the Purveyor-General in distributing supplies of all kinds, forwarded to him from head-quarters, and from various towns and cities in the Dominion. I also suggested important alterations in the ration list of the Field Force, such as a more liberal supply of fresh meat and compressed vegetables, and the substitution of oatmeal and molasses for a portion of the hard tack ration. Dr. Boyd took some trouble to find out the circumstances of the wounded men in Hospital, and assisted many of the more deserving by distributing clothing and small sums of money. He also kindly supplemented the ordinary allowance for travelling expenses, so that, instead of taking rations on their journey homeward, the men could pay for three meals a day. In this connection I would especially mention the case of a young Scout, Herbert Perrin, who had lost his arm, and who was anxious to visit his mother in a distant part of the country, and return to his homestead in the Territories. Dr. Boyd very kindly furnished him with fifty dollars from the fund in order to accomplish his object.

June 15th.—Being anxious to return to Saskatoon, and also give Dr. Boyd an opportunity of visiting the Field Hospital there, I left with him for Qu'Appelle to-day, and there took the trail for Clarke's Crossing. I chose this route because it was reported to be in excellent condition, and, furthermore, I wished Dr. Body to see the main trail to the front. We reached Saskatoon at 5 a. m. on the 18th.

Surgeon Bell reported all doing well, with the exception of Gunner Charpentier of "A" Battery, whose leg had required amputation, and who died a few days before. I at once began to make arrangements for the removal of all those remaining in the Hospital here, and in a despatch to the General suggested the river route by the way of the "Forks" and Lake Winnipeg. He concurred fully in my scheme, and instructed me to make the necessary arrangements, promising the assistance of one of the steamers.

June 24.—In reply to my telegram asking for instructions regarding the custody of the wounded Half-breed Delorme, Major-General Middleton replied as follows :—

"He must be kept under sentry and taken with you with the other wounded "and left at Regina. I will tell Col. Williams at Clarke's Crossing to send you a "guard when you think it necessary. Delorme is an important prisoner and must "not be allowed to escape."

I lost no time in communicating with Col. Williams, and suggested that it would be much safer and more convenient to take the prisoner to his camp, which he accordingly did.

June 25.—Sent five convalescent wounded to Moosejaw by trail, eighteen remaining.

Fearing that there might be some detention at Grand Rapids, I telegraphed to Lieut.-Col. Whitehead as follows :—

"Please instruct North-West Navigation Co. to facilitate movement of wound- "ed over tramway at Grand Rapids and on steamer. Some of wounded too weak to "leave their beds. D.'. Bell and Capt. Tracy in charge. Can you arrange to have "their wishes carried out by the Company's officers? Most important so as to have "no accident."

He replied :—

"Steamer 'Princess' leaves to-night for Grand Rapids to meet barge with "wounded. Captain will see that wounded are carefully conveyed across portage. "Every arrangement for care and comfort."

I also telegraphed Col. Whitehead to send to Grand Rapids from Winnipeg,— fresh meat, eggs, compressed vegetables, comforts, etc., so that the wounded might be kept well supplied with these necessaries.

Having decided to utilize a barge for purpose of transportation, obtained permission from Lieut.-Col. Whitehead to take possession of the best among the number lying at Clarke's Crossing, and proceeded to get it fitted up. Through the kindness of Col. Williams of the 7th Fusiliers, I secured the valuable services of Capt. Tracy of that regiment, and as many mechanics as the latter required. Capt. Tracy being an engineer, and a practical man, at once drew plans which satisfied me perfectly and lost no time in putting them into execution. The following report addressed to yourself has been kindly furnished by Capt. Tracy, referring to the mode of construction, capacity and qualifications generally of our Hospital Barge:—

LONDON, April 21, 1886.

D. BERGIN, ESQ., M.P.,
    Surgeon-General, Department Militia and Defence, Canada.

SIR,

I have the honor to report on the "Hospital Barge" used for the conveyance of wounded from Saskatoon down the Saskatchewan River on the way to Winnipeg.

The barge was selected from those built at Saskatchewan Landing for the conveyance of supplies to Clarke's Crossing, and on which the 7th Fusiliers and two Companies of the Midland Battalion made the trip down, about 320 miles.

I selected from the number the one with the best record on the down trip, and called the "Sir John A. Macdonald" (an omen of success), and with willing help from men of the 7th, proceeded to fix it up.

The barge was of pine about 16 x 50 feet, the bottom flat, turned up a little at the ends and of two inch plank, well caulked, the sides 2 inch plank and about 2 ft. 6 ins. high. About 4 feet at each end was decked over to strengthen the hull.

The inside of the hull was first thoroughly cleaned out, scrubbed and whitewashed. We then put in a new floor and additional cross timbers to strengthen the bottom, the sides were double-planked and a light strong frame put up to carry the covering and which added a good deal to the stiffness of the craft.

The covering was of canvas, securely battened to the frame with an inner ceiling to check the heat of the sun. The sides were canvas inside and outside, the frame fixed with cords to each, so that they could be tied up at any height desired, in fine weather.

The ends next the decked portions were enclosed with canvas, arranged to allow for thorough ventilation. Other little details were arranged, and, considering the materials available, the barge was very comfortable.

The cots were arranged, feet inwards, with a passage down the centre, some of the most serious cases being curtained off from the rest. The barge being used exclusively for the wounded, they were away from the noise and bustle of the steamer, an advantage of consequence in taking care of them.

The steamer "Alberta" arrived at the Crossing on the 3rd day of July, and towed the barge up the river to Saskatoon, where the wounded to the number of eighteen, were taken on board, and early next morning we returned to the Crossing, where two sick men of the 7th were added to the number. Dr. Fraser, Surgeon of the 7th, also joined us, and we proceeded down the river. Batoche was reached in the afternoon, where we stopped to take in wood, allowing such of the wounded as could walk to revisit the scene of the fighting. We stopped for the night near the "Hudson Bay Crossing" and reached the Forks of the River about noon, where we found A Company of the Midland Battalion. We waited here several days till General Middleton and the Troops coming down the North Branch arrived, when the whole started down the river.

Our steamer, being small, and having the Hospital Barge on one side, a double barge containing the Midland Co. on the other side, and a large barge in front for wood, cows, etc., was slower than the other, and we were soon left behind, but every night the General with the steamer "Marquis" waited for us to come up to see how the wounded were progressing.

On arriving at Cedar Lake, the wounded were transferred to the "Marquis," and the last I saw of our barge, which had served so well, was stripped of everything moveable; it was left at a little Indian village with a crowd of wondering Indians carefully examining it.

Our barge behaved well during the trip. A little water leaked in, the first day, through the upper joints from the wave in front, but we soon stopped that with a little oakum which we had brought along. The weather at the Forks was very disagreeable, being rainy most of the time. A second covering of canvas borrowed from the steamer helped to make the roof tight, and with the exception of the first night, we had no trouble. The barge rode smoothly and easily, being free from the jar of the machinery during the day, and the never-to-be-forgotten snoring of "Captain Maloney" at night.

On arriving at Grand Rapids, the wounded were taken across the tramway and placed on board of the "Princess," and after a very pleasant trip down the lake they were again transferred to a river steamer at Selkirk, and from there to Winnipeg, and by carriages and ambulances to the Hospital.

No accidents occurred on the trip, and the wisdom of sending the wounded in this way was undoubted. In the state of the trail from Saskatoon to the C. P. R. at Moosejaw, I do not think it would have been possible to have taken them over alive. As it was, they all seemed to improve very much on the trip, and I was confirmed in the opinion expressed above by the remarks of the men on seeing them at the Hospital, that they suffered more in being carried by road from the river to the Hospital than in the other 1100 miles by water. I might add that the care and skill shown by the Medical Department in preparing for and the looking after the wounded on the way, reflected the greatest credit on the Deputy Surgeon-General, Dr. Roddick, Dr. Bell, the Surgeon in charge, and his assistants and nurses.

I have the honor to be, Sir,

Your obedient servant,

THOMAS H. TRACY,

Captain 7th Fusiliers.

July 1.—All is now in readiness for evacuating Saskatoon Field Hospital, and we eagerly look for the arrival of the steamer. Being Dominion Day the occasion was celebrated as become loyal Canadians; the officers and men of the 7th Battalion kindly assisting in organizing games and amusements of all kinds for the benefit of the wounded.

July 3, 9 a.m.—The steamer "Alberta" arrived, towing the Hospital Barge taken on at Clarke's Crossing.

Arrangements were at once made for the removal of all the inmates of the Hospital to the barge, which was constructed to hold twenty beds.

Surgeon-Major Bell and Assistant-Purveyor Willoughby, with the dressers and nurses were quartered in the state-rooms and cabin of the steamer.

Two milch cows, and a liberal supply of fresh meat, vegetables, comforts, etc., were placed on board for the journey.

Dr. Boyd, who had manifested a deep interest in the men lying in the Saskatoon Hospital, supplied several whose clothing had been destroyed or lost with suits of serviceable corduroy, while others were tendered various sums of money so as to enable them to purchase comforts on the way home.

The steamer left during the night. I append the following report of Surgeon-Major Bell, giving the details of the journey from Saskatoon to Selkirk, via the Saskatchewan River and Lake Winnipeg :

WINNIPEG, July 16th, 1885.

T. G. RODDICK, Esq.,
　　　　Deputy Surgeon-General,
　　　　　　Militia of Canada, Montreal.

SIR,

I beg to submit the following report of the transport of the wounded from Saskatoon (and two or three others admitted to Hospital en route). Seventeen patients were put on board a barge specially prepared for the purpose on the night of the 3rd inst. The barge was lashed alongside the steamer "Alberta," and on board the latter were four nurses, one servant woman, three dressers, Dr. Willoughby (with the balance of the Saskatoon Equipment) and myself. On another barge were two cows and a man to look after them.

We sailed at daylight (July 4). At Clarke's Crossing we took on Dr. Fraser, 7th Fusiliers, Capt. Tracey, 7th Fusiliers (who had superintended the construction of the barge), and two privates of the same regiment, Pte. Dignam, suffering from abscess of back, and Pte. McClintock, acute rheumatism.

The patients were all very comfortable on board the barge, and we had a pleasant sail and good weather, reaching the "Forks" on Sunday morning, July 5th, about nine o'clock. Here we waited until Wednesday evening, July 8th, when General Middleton with the Troops from Pitt arrived in the "Marquis," "North-West" and "Baroness."

We sailed again at daylight, the "Marquis" keeping us in sight. We also took on here Pte. Hope Hay (Boulton's Horse), wounded in forearm at Batoche, and M. Vining of the Transport Service, also wounded at Batoche—flesh wound of thigh. Both were convalescent, and did not require beds in the Hospital Barge which was already full.

On Saturday afternoon we reached Cedar Lake, and after conferring with the General and the captains of both boats, we transferred the patients all to the "Marquis" the officers giving up their staterooms to them. On Sunday morning we reached Grand Rapids, and by evening had all transferred to the "Princess." On this boat the wounded occupied the ladies' cabin and two staterooms above. Several of the convalescents had beds made for them in the passage in front of and around the ladies' cabin. They were transferred by train across the neck of land (six miles I believe) without accident, and were very comfortable on the "Princess."

Here again Pte. Lemay, 65th Battalion, who was just convalescing from a bullet wound through chest, was admitted, and Pte. Warren, Q. O. R., with pleurisy. Just before starting, Pte. Bell, "Midland," was also admitted. He had obscure head symptoms, believed to have been produced by a fall from a barge at Clarke's Crossing. We crossed the lake without accident, two or three of the patients, and some of the nurses, suffering from sea-sickness, although the weather was fine.

On the morning of the 15th, we arrived with all well at Selkirk. Here Ptes. Lemay, Dignam and Bell were allowed to rejoin their regiments, to go on home with them.

Here, also, as you know, we transferred the others with attendants to the "Marquette," and arrived safely in Winnipeg at half-past six, and had all transferred to the Winnipeg Hospital by half-past eight p.m.

At the Forks, owing to the delay waiting for General Middleton, we were obliged to buy two small steers (all we could get) to provide fresh meat for the patients. At Grand Rapids most of our surplus supplies, drugs, mattrasses, etc., were left behind for further orders, as the boats were too crowded to carry them, and they were besides on the "Alberta," which had been detained by bad weather in Cedar Lake.

At the end of the voyage no one was the worse of the trip, and many I believe were much better for it. The transhipments were made without much or any discomfort to the patients, and no accidents occurred to any of them.

Captain Doucet had a slight fainting fit from keeping him too long in the upright position, going on board the "Princess," but was over it in a few minutes and was none the worse after.

I am Sir,

Your o'edient servant,

JAM'S B'L',

Surgeon in charge.

LIST OF SICK AND WOUNDED WHO LEFT SASKATOON FIELD HOSPITAL

On July 4, 1886, and took passage by boat to Winnipeg.

Captain Doucet, A. D. C.	Private Barton, Midland
Lieutenant Laidlaw, Midland.	" A. L. Young, 90th Battalion
" Garden, Intelligence Corps.	" Milson, G enadiers.
Corporal J. E. Lethbridge, 90th Battalion.	" Eager, "
Private Fairbanks, " A " Battery.	" A. Martin, "
Drummer Thos. Srout, "	" Cook, French's Scouts.
Private Dowker, 90th Battalion.	Trooper Thompson, Boulton's Scouts.
" Cantwell, Grenadiers.	McDonald, Settler.
" Daley, Midland.	

July 4th.—Reports having reached me to the effect that there were several Half-breeds wounded, lying ill and unattended about the districts of Fisk Creek and Batoche, I determined to visit these places before returning to the Base. Dr. Boyd was also anxious to see the battle fields, and carry out the instructions of Her Royal Highness, to render assistance to foes and friends indiscriminately. Accordingly, accompanied by Captain Leonard and Mr. A. D. Stewart, we started immediately after the departure of the steamer, reaching Fish Creek about noon that day; visited the house then occupied by Madame Touraud, her own dwelling having been destroyed during the engagement. I found one of her sons suffering from an affection of the lungs, which had been much increased by recent exposure. I gave him the necessary advice and medicine. Then we proceeded to Batoche and put up for the night at Batoche's house, where we were warmly welcomed.

The following morning we visited the priest, and learned from him that the wounded in his parish, numbering in all about ten, were mostly convalescent. He asked me however to see a Half-breed named Gardupuy, who had been wounded through the lung. After some trouble I found him, because he feared arrest, and on examination discovered that he had a chest filled with fluid. I did not feel justified in operating under the circumstances, but gave him a letter to the police surgeon at Prince Albert, assuring him that every attention would be paid him. Dr. Boyd kindly furnished him with the means necessary to get there. I left with the priest a stock of dressings, bandages, etc., and Dr. Boyd presented him with a considerable sum of money to be distributed among the sick and destitute in his parish.

Returned to Saskatoon on the 7th, and spent a couple of days closing accounts with the settlers, and shipping by trail goods of various kinds, which the steamer had been unable to carry. I then proceeded to the base, reaching Moosejaw by trail on the 10th July.

I found the Base Hospital closed, in obedience to your instructions, the staff, with the exception of Purveyor-General Sullivan, having gone on to Winnipeg, with orders to proceed home. I pushed on to Winnipeg, so as to be in readiness to meet the wounded on their arrival there.

July 15.—Major-General Middleton, with Troops and wounded, arrived at Selkirk this morning, all well. The steamer "Marquette" was in readiness, under my orders, to receive the wounded, who were accordingly transferred directly from the "Princess," the steamers being moored together.

Dr. Kerr awaited the arrival of the steamer at Winnipeg, having a number of comfortable waggons provided, in which the men were taken to the Winnipeg General Hospital.

I found all the wounded looking better for the journey, and it is gratifying to be able to state that all the transhipments were made without the slightest accident.

The next three or four days were fully occupied in Winnipeg, paying off the Field Hospital Corps, drafting the wounded men home, etc.

It was my intention to have returned to Moosejaw, where several claims in connection with our Department awaited settlement, but on July 22nd I received an order from the Minister to return home, leaving Purveyor-General Sullivan to close the accounts, etc.

Aug. 3.—Accompanied by Dr. Boyd, reported to you at Ottawa. At your suggestion, and with the concurrence of the Minister, I subsequently returned to the North West (leaving Ottawa Aug. 10), for the purpose of assisting the Commissariat Officers stationed there in the settlement of accounts, having special reference to our Department. I travelled along the line of railway, as far as Calgary, settling all claims presented. I am convinced that in this way much trouble and expense, besides costly litigation, were saved to the Department. Returned August 31, 1885.

I think it must be conceded on all sides that the campaign on the whole has been a most successful one. It is difficult to conceive any expeditionary force similarly equipped and circumstanced coming out of such an ordeal in such good form and with so few losses. The Canadian Volunteer has proved himself to be a soldier of no mean order. His powers of endurance and fortitude, whether confronting the enemy or in the hospital ward, have been thoroughly tested and found not wanting. Again, the remarkable rapidity with which wounds healed, and the very small mortality of sick and wounded, go far to prove the excellent physique of the men and their extraordinary powers of recuperation.

It affords me much pleasure to put on record my high appreciation of the valuable services of the medical staff engaged in the campaign. Where so many are distinguished it is difficult to individualize,* but it may be safely said that as a body they have shown themselves to be devoted, self-sacrificing, unflinching in the face of danger, and, where occasion offered, prompt and able surgeons. I desire to acknowledge their cordial co-operation on all occasions, my anxieties and responsibilities having been considerably lightened thereby.

The dressers and orderlies attached to the different columns and hospitals also deserve mention. During the engagements at Batoche and Cut Knife Hill, more especially, they are reported by the respective Brigade Surgeons to have done excellent service, and in some cases to have displayed undoubted bravery in removing the wounded from exposed places in the field. In the case of those attached to the Hospital at Saskatoon I can testify to their unwearied attention to duty.

The Commissariat and Quartermaster Departments are justly entitled to our thanks for their prompt and efficient aid in furnishing supplies and transportation. To the Major-General Commanding we owe a debt of gratitude for his uniform kindness and consideration. His constant care of the soldiers serving under him and his untiring solicitude for the wounded are now proverbial. Where the comfort or safety of the latter was concerned he was never slow in granting a request.

In conclusion, I may be excused for saying that if my work in connection with the recent campaign in the North West has been performed to the satisfaction of the Minister and yourself it is due in great measure to the hearty co-operation and support which you have both extended to me. Without them I must have signally failed in many particulars. The excellent selection which you personally made of supplies of various kinds and the prompt manner in which they were placed at the disposal of the Purveyor-General tended not a little to lessen my anxieties and added materially to the well-being and comfort of our sick and wounded men.

I have the honor to be, Sir,

Your obedient servant,

T. G. RODDICK,
Deputy Surgeon-General.

---

* Here, however, I cannot refrain from specifying the valuable services of Dr. Bell, whom I recalled from the front to take charge of the hospital at Saskatoon. For a time his was one of the most responsible positions in the force, having some eighty sick and wounded men under his care.

(E).—REPORT OF PURVEYOR-GENERAL, HON. DR. SULLIVAN.

OTTAWA, May 11, 1886.

SIR,

In compliance with your request, I have the honor to submit a brief resumé of the operations of the Purveyor's Department N.W. Forces during the late Rebellion. I regret very much that, being almost entirely drawn from memory, it will not be as minute as it should. I have, however, sent so many reports and letters that I may refer to them for full and complete details of every transaction.

I arrived in Winnipeg on the 9th of April. After reporting immediately to Col. Jackson, who expressed his entire ignorance of my position and duties, or even the existence of such a Department as had been entrusted to me, I reported to the Deputy Surgeon-General, Dr. Roddick, and called on Dr. Douglas.

I accompanied Dr. Douglas to the C. P. Railway stores, and looked at the four sets of medical outfit, each set consisted of a large number of boxes or small cases, containing medicine, medical appliances, and instruments. I proposed to check them, but he declined, on the ground of want of time, also, " there was no necessity." He said he would take two sets with him, and I could send on the remaining, as he required them ; there was no use opening nor examining them.

The following day I removed the goods to a convenient store, rented for the purpose, and opened and examined them. I was surprised at the selection, and the quantity so different from what I thought required. I have reported fully on them, their quality, price, etc. I then used every means in my power to inform the Surgeons of the different corps of my desire and ability to supply their wants. Many applied, some were doubtful, while a few positively refused and " would buy their supplies." I was the more anxious to notify them, because I was asked and refused to pass an account of nearly $500 incurred by a Surgeon of a battalion for instruments, medicines and appliances, out of all reason, and sufficient for several regiments. It also surprised me to find so many Surgeons coming up with their corps entirely, or almost entirely, destitute of the commonest instruments and appliances required in every-day work.

I examined Major White's Company of Scouts, and visited the Hospital in addition to my other duties. I knew the solicitude of the Surgeon-General, to provide hospital accommodation, and when I received your message to that effect, viz., to establish one, I examined carefully all the available localities and buildings in the town. I saw that the Winnipeg Hospital was new, clean and well attended, equal to the best in Canada, and had been informed by Dr Roddick that he had made an arrangement at $1.50 per diem for each soldier, to be paid Surgeon and Assistant Surgeon. While I was most anxious to carry out your suggestion, or rather orders, and inclined to your views strongly, still I hesitated to accept the great responsibility and expense, and urged, as being much the best, the arrangement of Dr. Roddick, at the same time recommending a vigilant inspection.

I was engaged daily in giving supplies to the different Battalion Surgeons, they were granted on requisitions duly signed; they required, according to your orders, the signature of the Deputy Surgeon-General. Very few of them had it, because that officer was not often on the same station with me, and it would be foolish to wait for him, otherwise they were all duly signed. On the day following the battle of Batoche a public meeting of the citizens of Winnipeg was held, at which, by request, I was present. I informed the meeting of the solicitude of the Government, and the abundance of necessary comfort in my charge, the only difficulty was that of transport,—that I had several boxes ready to go forward and all I asked was their aid to send them. I was enabled to send them on the next day. I had also the honor of transmitting to you the generous offer of the Sisters of St Boniface to nurse the sick and wounded, and also the offer of the ladies of Winnipeg to send seven volunteer trained nurses at once. The next day a car filled with supplies arrived from Ottawa or Montreal addressed to me; the railway officials refused to let me have it without an order from Col. Jackson, Chief Supply Officer. On application to Colonel Jackson he refused, saying he had no authority or orders to recognize me. I appealed to him, in view of the urgency, and offered to give my own bonds, but in vain, until I wrote him, disclaiming any further responsibility and transferring it to him. When the order was issued, I had no fault to find with Col. Jackson, who treated me always very courteously, but attributed it to his not having received any orders. I may be permitted to state here the obligations I was under to the Superintendent, Mr. Egan, the Deputy Superintendent, Mr. Shields, and all the officials of the Canadian Pacific Railway, for many acts of kindness, and I can bear cheerful testimony to their zeal in forwarding all the supplies with promptitude and care, always good-natured and agreeable. I never applied to them in vain, and they could not have done better if for themselves.

I frequently asked for letters of credit and authority to purchase goods, but did not receive a satisfactory reply. I could not, therefore, pay the hotel and other expenses of dressers and surgeons which I was asked to do. They were constantly arriving and going forward, and were much dissatisfied when I could not pay their bills.

On the 1st of May I received orders to proceed to Swift Current, and lost no time in packing up our stores, filled two cars and part of another. On my arrival at Swift Current, I found the hospital car used as a dormitory by dressers, orderlies and surgeons, while the caboose was used as a dwelling by the Commandant General Laurie, and the Surgeon in command of the Hospital Corps. On further examination, I found that an old dirty, dilapidated car, deeply imbedded in the mud, was used as a hospital. It was close to the Railway latrines, the odors from which it could not escape; there were two or three sick soldiers in this, and they were attended by 19 (nineteen) dressers and 4 surgeons. I immediately determined to make a change, and had two marquees or hospital tents and four small ones pitched on an elevated situation, and had the patients removed. I wrote out a set of rules and regulations, a copy of which I submitted to you for approval; tin stoves were put up as the nights were very cold; I had more than once to procure wood, and prepare it, and gave my own blankets to a patient, which were never returned. I mention these things to show the difficulties I had to contend with. In addition I had to look after the stores, and ship as quickly as possible the orders which came from different sources. Our great difficulty here and all through the Rebellion was the want of means of transport; had I not taken great pains to secure it, very little would have been sent. I also ordered the hospital car to be cleaned, and ready to start at any moment during our stay. One man died, named Marais, he had had heart disease, and was left in Hospital by the 9th when they left. No post mortem was held, the body was embalmed and sent to Calgary.

From Swift Current detachments were being constantly sent to different points, and each of these requiring a surgeon, dressers and outfit, the number of surgeons and dressers were soon diminished, and having fewer in number at the Hospital it was better attended, and soon became as perfect as a hospital situated where it was could possibly be. When I was beginning to feel proud of the Hospital, we were suddenly ordered to Moosejaw. On the twentieth (20th) of May, I immediately ordered the car for the sick to be put in readiness. We transferred the patients to it without any difficulty; they were very comfortable, very well attended to, and were removed without a single complaint.

General Laurie had previously selected buildings (a number of which were vacant) for hospital offices and stores; the store for me was too small, and I had to engage another to protect the goods. A Base Hospital was established here. All being comfortably settled, and Dr. Roddick being in charge, I, as you had ordered a short time previously, undertook to make a tour of inspection as far as Calgary, visiting Medicine Hat, in charge of Dr. Tobin of the 9th, Crowfoot in charge of Dr. Cloutier, and Calgary in charge of Dr. Tracy—the latter, the largest, I recommended be closed, and Dr. Tracy with his outfit removed to Moosejaw; after a day or two this was done. I found everything working satisfactorily and no complaints. Of this visit I submitted a full report. Soon after our removal to Moosejaw, the Superior and 4 sisters of St. John arrived, from Toronto, in charge of Dr. Canniff. As might be expected, their services were of great value, they established order, regularity and vigilance, and won the respect and affection of all. We received, from time to time, wounded and sick who could be carried from Saskatoon. Boards of examination were held. Agreeably to the orders of the Surgeon-General, several of these I attended, and in every case those who requested to be sent there, and in fact all, were made to understand that any further surgical or medical assistance required by them would not be at the expense of the Government. Many were sent to Winnipeg Hospital who had resided in that locality; contracts were made for washing. As the patients were gradually convalescing, and the Saskatoon patients were to be removed with the troops by water to Winnipeg, I was enabled with your authority, to close the Hospital, on the 20th of June. I regret to say it was left in a filthy condition, some goods missing were said to have been burned for sanitary reasons, without my knowledge; some few were broken or lost, and the remainder sold by auction. I received from you orders for the final disposition of the goods in my charge. These were to sell a portion, to store a portion, and to bring a portion home; these instructions were faithfully executed.

The new and choice goods, likely to be required for Government service in the future, I had carefully packed in Col. Peebles' store, and we have his receipt therefor. The remaining portion, viz., instruments and valuable drugs, were carefully packed by Mr. Tobin, brought home and handed over to you. I visited the Winnipeg Hospital daily, when Dr. Roddick was absent; I also attended Examining Boards, and, on the 31st of July, sent you a full statement of the history, present condition, and probable results of each case.

From Dr. Willoughby, acting as Purveyor at Saskatoon, I received the store remaining from that Hospital. On the 11th July, having arranged everything satisfactorily, we packed up and left for Winnipeg. I reported fully on these goods, their condition, as well as my examination of some of the accounts of the Hospital at Saskatoon.

A few days after, I returned home with the goods, as ordered by you. As you are aware, sir, I had to forward all parcels sent by friends to their relatives and friends in the North-West. Troublesome and unpleasant as it proved to be it was faithfully done. Unfortunately, I had no authority to pay any charges due when they reached me, and regretted I could not send them on promptly. When such was not the case, they were sent on the first opportunity which offered. To me also was entrusted the receipt and distribution of the donations and gifts from cities ladies' societies. This added very largely to our work; it was equal almost to my proper work, and entailed great labor and anxiety. Still it was agreeable, the labor seemed a pleasure. Were it otherwise, it could not have been done, because, as you know, I had only one assistant and no outside help.

The department being a new one, there was difficulty in having it recognized and its importance estimated. I have often asked the issue of an order to those concerned, of the necessity of communicating with us. In many instances, Surgeons refused to deliver up the medical stores in their possession. This condition was, no doubt, largely due to the existence of two medical organizations, the one Regimental, the other, a separate Army Medical Department. I may remark, that experience and close observation made me a strong supporter of the latter. Under the direction of a good head, harmony and a high state of efficiency can be readily secured by the latter. The failure of the Regimental service to at all meet the requirements of the Rebellion could not be more fully shown. Had it not been for the Staff Surgeons, the complaints would have been many, severe and grievous. I have not time nor occasion to discuss it at length, but, I think I can easily prove by my experience, the superior advantages of a separate Army Medical Department.

In my opinion, too many dressers were sent; they did not prove equal to the trained female nurse, and could, if not dispensed with altogether, be reduced to a very small number. I also strongly recommend that the Surgeon in charge should be responsible for the management of his hospital or ward, and accountable for instruments, appliances, etc., supplied to him. It is impossible for a Purveyor to take charge of articles that are in the hands of others, and discharge his other duties.

Many other suggestions I could make, but this is not the occasion. If a special inquiry be made, I will gladly give my opinions, if required. I believe we should not lose an experience so peculiar and varied.

The plan of a separate Army Medical Department was wise and beneficial; its defects were few and readily remedied. I can honestly congratulate you, sir, on an efficiency which elicited the approbation of all. All that the most improved modern science could suggest was furnished, and in a liberal manner.

The number of requisitions filled shows how extensively the supplies were distributed ; it would have been much greater had facilities for transport been present.

When to so much care on the part of the Government, we add the munificence and generosity of the ladies of the Dominion—prominent among whom were those of Montreal and Niagara Falls—we need not wonder that those most interested, viz., the sick and wounded, expressed not only sentiments of satisfaction, but of astonishment and admiration.

With the assurance of my gratitude for your courtesy and consideration,

I have the honor to be,

Your obedient servant,

M. SULLIVAN.

To Dr. D. BERGIN, M.P.,
Surgeon-General, &c., &c.

(F).—LIST OF PENSION BOARDS.

Extract from Militia General Orders.

HEAD QUARTERS,

OTTAWA, 16th October, 1885.

GENERAL ORDERS (23).
No. 1.

MEDICAL BOARDS.

The following Gentlemen have been appointed to form Medical Boards at the stations indicated, for the purpose of investigating claims on the part of Active militiamen in the respective districts, who received wounds or injuries, or contracted disease while on service in the North-West Territories during the recent Rebellion, which may incapacitate them wholly or in part from following their usual occupation :—

Military District No. 1.

London.

Dr. Veasy A. Brown,   President.
Dr. Alex. Fenwick,   } Members.
Dr. Chas. G. Moore, Sr., }

Military District No. 2.

Toronto.

Dr. Henry Hover Wright,   President.
Dr. James Hepburn Burns, } Members.
Dr. R. A. Pyne,   }

Military District No. 3.

Kingston.

Dr. Fife Fowler,   President.
Dr. Benj. F. Wilson,   } Members.
Dr. George H. Boulter,   }

Military District No. 4.

Ottawa.

Dr. James A. Grant, Sr.,   President.
Dr. Robt. H. W. Powell, } Members.
Dr. Léandre C. Prevost,   }

Military District Nos. 5 and 6.

Montreal.

Dr. Geo. E. Fenwick,   President.
Dr. J. Guerin,   }
Dr. L. Edouard Desjardins, } Members.
Dr. Gilbert P. Girdwood,   }

Military District No. 7.

Quebec.

Dr. Colin Sewell,   President.
Dr. Laurent Catellier,   } Members.
Dr. Eutrope E. Dionne,   }

D

Military District No. 10.

Winnipeg.

Honorable Dr. J. O'Donnell,   President.

Dr.   Lynch, ⎫
Dr. Donald Henderson, ⎬ Members.
Dr. Theigòne Fafard, ⎭

The cases to be investigated are divided into two classes:—

1st. Cases of militiamen who have received wounds or injuries, or have contracted disease on actual service, such as to incapacitate them wholly from following their usual trade or profession.

2nd. Cases of militiamen who have received wounds or injuries, or have contracted disease, on actual service, such as to incapacitate them for a time from following their usual trade or profession.

The Boards will take such evidence as may be produced, and will report their own opinions thereupon, either as to the total or partial disability of the claimant ; if the disability is partial, the Board will state the amount of injury or incapacity under which the claim ant is suffering at the date of the investigation, and its probable duration. The opinion of the Board will, of course, be based solely on the evidence which is embodied in the "Proceedings," which must be according to the form prescribed by the paragraph 1006 of the Regulations and Orders for the Militia, 1883.

The Board will assemble on such days as may in their opinion be necessary for the purpose of investigating the claims which are laid before them by the Deputy Adjutant General of their district. Each member of a Board will receive Surgeon's pay for the days he is present, and in the discharge of his duties on the Board. The claims for such pay to be certified by the President.

Each case is to be investigated separately. The "Proceedings" in each completed case are to be forwarded with as little delay as possible to the Deputy Adjutant General of the District, in order that they may be produced as evidence before the Board of Officers specified in paragraph 1008 of the Regulations and Orders, 1883.

By Command,

WALKER POWELL, Colonel,

Adjutant General of Militia,

Canada.

(G.)—HOSPITAL SUPPLIES.

LIST OF FURNITURE, UTENSILS, HOSPITAL CLOTHING, BEDDING, MEDICAL AND SURGICAL APPLIANCES, INSTRUMENTS AND MEDICAL COMFORTS, TO BE OBTAINED FROM THE PURVEYOR AT WINNIPEG UPON REQUISITION DULY MADE AND COUNTERSIGNED AND APPROVED BY THE DEPUTY SURGEON-GENERAL.

BEDDING.

Blankets
Mattrasses
Air Beds
Sheets
Water Beds
Pillows
I. R. Pillows
Bolsters
I. R. Circulars
Pillow Slips
Bolster do
Palliasses
Cots, Folding
Stretchers, Folding
Towels
Hospital Chairs
Flags (red cross)

UTENSILS.

Baking Ovens
Bread Pans
Camp Stew Kettles
" Tea "
" Dippers
Camp Frying Pans
" Pudding "
Wrought Iron Hanger for Kettles
" " Slings
Camp Oil Stoves
Granite Iron Kettles for Oil Stoves
" " Sauce Pans, large
" " " " Windsor
Stove Wicks
Heating Fluid in Cans for Coal Oil Stoves
Galv. Iron Packing Cans for Stoves and Furniture
Wash Basins, G. I.
Water and Slop Buckets, G. I.
Knives and Forks
Teaspoons
Dessert Spoons

Table Spoons
Candlesticks
Butter Knives
Meat Saws
Buck Saws
Nail Hammers
Nails
Axes (long handles)
Meat Choppers
Can Openers
Cork Screws (pocket)
Chisels
Spades (Garden)
Shovels (pointed, long handles)
Measures gal, pint and ½ pint
Water Filters
Wash Tubs
Slates
Soup Ladles
Padlocks
Pencils
Clothes Pins
Clothes Lines
Bed Cord
Water Bottles with Cup and Strap
Bath Sponges
I. R. Vapour Bath
Salt Cellars
Pepper Casters
Screw Drivers
Cups and Saucers
Soup Bowls
Plates (Dinner)
Plates (Soup)
Dishes (Dinner)
Tea Pots
Coffee Pots
Tarpaulin

CLOTHING.

Men's Woolen Stockings
Men's Carpet Slippers

LIST OF MEDICINES, MEDICAL APPARATUS, SURGICAL APPLIANCES, MEDICAL
COMFORTS AND NECESSARIES, TO BE OBTAINED ON REQUISITION TO THE PURVEYOR AT WINNIPEG.

MEDICINES.

Acid, Carbolic
    Gallic
    Nitric
    Sulphuric
    Tartaric
Ammonia Carbonas
Antimon Tart
Argenti Nitras
Atropia Sulph. Solut
Ammon Aromatic Spts.
Camphor
Chloral Hydras
Chloroform in lb. bots.
Collodion
Creasoti
Cupri-Sulph.
Chlorodyne
Canada Balsam
Copaiva
Ether Sulph. (Squibbs)
Ether Nitrosi Spts.
Elixir Eucalyptus
Ext. Hyoxyanni Spt.
Ext. Fluid Nuc Vomic
Ext. Fluid Scillæ
Empl. Resinœ
Ext. Fluid Tolu
Ext. Fl. Podophyllin
    " Belladonna
    " Gentian
    " Cardam
    " Catechu
Ext. Fl. Cinnamon
    " Hyoscyami
    " Ergot .
    " Digitalis
    " Jaborandi
Ferri Sulphas
Tr Benzoin Co.
Tr Capsici
Glycerine
Hydrarg sub. chlor.
Hydrarg fort Ung.
Iodine (pure)

Opii Pulv.
Pill Ague, Improved
Pill Aloin comp.
Pill Cathartic
Pill Copaiba & Ext. Cubeb
Pill Digitalis comp.
Pill Ext. cannab Indic
Pill Gonorrhœa
Pill Iodoform and Hydrarg
Pill Dover (Ipecac and opium)
Pill Ferri Citrat & Strychn
Pill Morph. Sulph.
Pill Morph Atrop No. 2
Pill Neuralgic (Nelaton's)
Pill Opium & Acct. Plumb No. 1
Pill Pepsin Bism & Strychn
Pill Phosphorus & Ext. Cannabis Indic
Pill Phosphorus Iron & Nux. Vomica.
Pill Salicylic
Pill Syphilitic
Pill Blue
Potash Iod.
Quinæ Sulph
Sodæ Bicarb
Strychniæ Sol. B. P.
Tr. Opii Camph.
Vaseline
Zinci Sulph
Zinci Chlorat
Zinci Oxid

APPLIANCES.

Basins
Corks, Phial
Corks, Pints
Corks, Quarts
Cushions, Air
Ipecac Vin.
Ipecac Pulv.
Lig Ammon : fort
Magnesia Sulph.
Morph. Hydrochlor
Morph. Tablets ·
Ol Olivæ or Papaveris
    " " Ricini
    " " Terebinth

Funnels, Tin
Gutta Percha (thick)
Gutta Percha (Tissue)
Cotton Corded in Rolls
Grey Cotton for bandages
Borated A. C. Cotton
Graduated Measures Glass
Paper Wrapping
Pencils, Camel Hair
Pestle and Mortar Wedgewood
Phials, Common assorted
Powder Boxes
Pins, ordinary Packets
Pins, Safety
Scales and Weights
Scissors (Shop)
Silk Ligature
Dif. Sizes Catgut Carbolized
Large Rolls Rubber Plaster, Scabury and
  Johnsons
Splints, common
Slab (Wedgewood)
Spatula
Sponges
Spongio Piline
Tape, (broad)
Tape (narrow)
Thermometer Clinical
Tow, Antiseptic
Tubing, India rubber
Urinals, pewter
Weights spare (grains)
Wires, silver, for sutures

NECESSARIES.

Brooms
Candles or lamps, Tin or Iron
Flannel (red)
Matches, ordinary
Sewing needles, assorted
Poultice material, mustard
  "   "   Linseed meal
Twine, strong
Lamps
Coal Oil Stove

INSTRUMENTS.*

Bullet Forceps
Dresser's Forceps
Tooth Forceps

Forceps (bone)
Forceps (artery)
Bougies, Gum Elastic
Catheters, Silver Male
Catheters, Gum Elastic
Bucks Weights
D Needles, Suture, mixed
Lancets
Pocket Dressing Cases
Probes, ordinary
  "   bullet
Stomach Pump
Stethoscopes, metal
Scissors, straight
  "   curved
Syringes, Hypodermic
Syringes, I. R.
Tourniquets
Plaster of Paris
Nitrat Silver, pocket holder

MEDICAL COMFORTS.

Essence of Beef
Corn Starch
Tea
Sugar
Wine, Sherry in quarts.
Whiskey, Rye, quarts
Brandy in cases, quarts
Porter (Guinness), pints
Candles, sperm or wax
Mustard, ¼ Tins
Pepper (ground)
Salt, Glass Jars
Vegetables in Tins, desiccated
Turnips
Mixed Vegetables }
Potatoes
Soap, Common Yellow Bar.
Soap, Castile Bars
Condensed Milk (In tins)
Dried fruit in Cans
W. W. Vinegar
Cayenne Pepper
Barley (Pearl)
Rice
Coffee (Ground) in Tins
Cocoa

* All these instruments to be issued only on repayment.

Whiskey Rye (brl)
Biscuits (Abernethy)
Canned Meats
 "   Fruits
Oranges
Lemons

SUPPLEMENTARY.

Sick Feeders
Spitting Cups
Tumblers
Water Pitchers
Carvers and Forks
Butchers' Steels
Bread Knives
Crockery drinking Cups
Chambers
Water Cans

Close Stools
Bed Pans
Urinals
Bath Tubs, foot and large
Table Cloths
Eye Napkins
Butcher Knives
Croton Oil
Handbaskets
Lemon Squeezers
Hair Brushes
Combs, Dressing
Combs, F. Tooth
Scrubbers
Grocers' Scales and Weights
Punchees
Water-Proof Sheets, white

(H.)—MEDICAL TRANSPORT CART.

REQUISITES.

1st. To be large enough to carry three (3) boxes for stores, each 18 inches wide, 36 inches long, and 18 inches high.

2nd. The weight of the finished cart, with wheels and empty boxes, must not exceed 600 lbs., and have strength of frame sufficient to withstand a load of 800 lbs.

3rd. The cart-wheels must be interchangeable with the hind wheels of the new ambulance wagon.

SPECIFICATIONS.

WHEELS.—The wheels will be 4 feet 2 inches high (without tires), the hubs (of best elm) 6½ inches in diameter at centre, 5½ inches at butt, and 4½ inches at the point, by 9 inches in length; butt with iron bands on each end mortised for sixteen (16) spokes. Size of mortise 1⅝ inches by 9-16 inch with a ⅞ inch disk. Spokes (best seasoned hickory) 1⅓ inches by ⅝ inch (hub tenon) felloe tenon, round ¾ inch in diameter; felloes (best hickory) 1⅝ inches, two (2) pieces for each wheel; tire (best charcoal iron) 1½ inches wide, by ⅜ inch thick, fastened on with eight (8) tire-bolts in each wheel; two (2) felloe-plates in each wheel over joints.

AXLE.—Of best quality refined iron 1½ inch square for 7 inches from each collar-washer, the remainder rounded. Collar-washer 2⅝ inches in diameter, ⅜ inch thick; wheel-boxes of best quality foundry iron, 7½ inches long, 1½ inches in diameter, 7-16 inch thick at butt; 1⅜ inches in diameter, and 5-16 inch thick at point, with two (2) lugs, 2 inches long, ½ inch high. Oil-chamber, 2 inches long, 1-16 inch deep, to commence 2½ inches from the butt. Weight of box, not less than 4¾ lbs. each. Axle to be arranged to track five feet from centre to centre of wheels.

BODY.—Outside length 57⅛ inches, width 40¼ inches, height 8 inches. Inside length 54⅞ inches, width 38 inches, height 6 inches. Frame, of oak, consisting of two (2) exterior side-sills and two (2) end cross-bars, size 1¼ by 2½ inches. Centre cross-bar 2 inches by ¾ inch, and two (2) interior cross-bars, at half distance between the centre and the ends, 2 inches by ¾ inch; all cross-bars, except the tail-bar, are mortised into the side-sills, and are even with them at bottom; the tail-bar is mortised to received the sill-tenons. The tenons of the end bars are of one-third thickness; those of the interior bars are of half the thickness. The floor planks will be ash, ½ inch thick, and level with the top of the side-sills. The upper rails are 1⅛ inches by 1 inch, and extend over the sides and front, and are vertical. The side panels of the body are of ash, screwed, each side, to six (6) single studs and to a front double corner stud; the front panel of the body, also of ash, ½ inch thick, is screwed in like manner, to three (3) single studs and the double corner studs, to which the sides are attached. These studs are all tenoned into the side sills and upper rails. The studs are 5 inches long; the single ones ¾ inch by 1 inch, and chamfered at their exterior corners between the sill and upper rail. The double corner studs are made from square pieces 1⅞ by 1½ inches. The sides and front of the body are stayed by upright rods and flat angle-irons about the front corners and the sides, so by upright and brace-rods at the rear. The ends of the rear cross-bar and the centre-bar project 4½ inches beyond each side to receive lower ends of these braces.

The tail-board is framed of $\frac{3}{8}$ inch (panel) boards of ash, screwed to five (5) studs $\frac{3}{4}$ by 1 inch, mortised into a top and bottom rail 1 inch by $1\frac{1}{2}$ inches. The length of tail-board extends even with the exterior of the sides. The tail-board will be hung to the rear cross-bar by three light hinges to stand even with the end of bar when upright, and will be hold closed by means of hooks attached to the sides, and hooking into eyes attached to the irons on the upper rail of the tail-board.

SPRINGS.—Two (2) side half-springs, perpendicular to the axle, and clipped beneath it, connected in front by a cross-spring. The side springs are to be 48 inches long, of English No. 3 oil-tempered steel, of five (5) leaves, 2 inches wide. The cross-spring, of the same number of leaves, of the same width and thickness and 38 inches long, or of sufficient length to connect the side-springs. The eye will be of double thickness, and have eye-bolts 7-16 of an inch. The spread of the springs should be as slight as will keep the body off the axle. The cross-spring will be bolted to an iron cross-piece, which is bolted to the shafts and side-sills. The side-springs will be clipped beneath the axle, by pairs of clips, screwed by nuts, with brass spring-blocks. Behind, the side-springs will be bolted to the sills by iron V-pieces, as may be found most convenient. India-rubber buffers may be interposed over the clips of the side-springs to the axle.

THE SHAFTS are made of ash, $1\frac{3}{4}$ by $2\frac{1}{4}$ inches, separated 22 inches in front and $30\frac{1}{2}$ inches at the foot-board. They will be somewhat curved, so as to carry the body nearly level, or with a slight inclination downwards at the rear. They are bolted to the body through the front-cross bar and the forward interior bars, being also locked by mortises $1\frac{1}{4}$ inches deep at each bolt. A foot-board 4 feet long 3 inches wide and 1 inch thick, of oak, is bolted to the top of the side-sills, which extend 8 inches in front of the body, to receive the foot-board. The bolts also pass through triangular blocks placed between the foot-board and the sills, and also on the shafts, which give a suitable inclination to the board.

SWINGLE-TREE AND SPLINTER-BAR.—The draft is made from the axle by means of two (2) wrought-iron rods $\frac{1}{2}$ inch in diameter, bolted under the foot-board to an oaken splinter-bar, to which the swingle-tree is attached. The swingle-tree will conform to that used in the ambulance wagon.

CHESTS.—There will be three (3) chests, interchangeable, and consequently of uniform dimensions, viz., 36 inches long, 18 inches wide, 18 inches high. They will be made of half-inch boards of walnut or ash, and firmly framed, and secured against splits or strains by light steel straps and angle braces. The bottoms of the boxes will be covered with sheet zinc, and the tops by cow-hide. The under corners will be supplied with strong castors, and at the middle of each end there will be strong iron folding-handles, which must not project more than half an inch when folded down. The chests will open from above by hinged-lids, and will be secured, each, by two suitable bolts and locks equidistant from either end.

SLIDE-BOARD.—A slide-board, to lower the boxes from the cart to the ground, will be carried on iron loops attached underneath the body, so that when drawn to the rear, to be used as a slide, the hooks at the front end will hold by the rear loops, and when not wanted for use this board will slide back on its loop, and be secured by a thumb-screw.

TARPAULIN.—A canvas cover, about $6\frac{1}{2}$ by 5 feet, will be provided with eyelets at the four corners, to be secured to suitable adjustable fastenings to the four corner studs.

PAINTING.—The cart will be painted of the color and finish of caissons and other ordnance carriages, the iron work black. The letters D. C., four inches high, will be painted at the centre of each side panel. Near the front end of each side panel a stencil mark will be placed with the inscription, in small characters, Transport Cart D. C. Med. Dept.

In carrying out this work, the endeavor has been made to select from the standard supply table of the Medical Department such medicines, stores, appliances and utensils as experience has proved to be useful and necessary for the ordinary emergencies of field service, and to arrange them compactly and conveniently.

As the supply table has been strictly conformed to in the preparation of the list for furnishing these chests, it will be possible to refurnish them from the stores usually found at even the more remote frontier posts. Under the circumstances ordinarily attendant upon scouts, expeditions, and marches, it is believed that the quantity and variety of the supply furnished will be abundantly adequate for a force of not less than five hundred troops for a period of three months. The medicine chest has been divided by means of accurately fitting trays into five divisions, the trays subdivided into spaces and compartments for the disposal of medicines, appliances, etc., and, so far as possible, these spaces and compartments have been constructed with reference to the average size and form of the original package or article furnished for the Medical Department, so that the chest may be readily and quickly filled from any dispensary.

MEDICINE CHEST.—The medicine chest is furnished with five trays covered by accurately fitting lids. The trays are of black walnut, and are seventeen and a half inches long, sixteen and three-quarter inches wide, and vary in depth and in their subdivisions.

All the trays are readily raised by apertures for the fingers cut near the upper edges of the ends.

Tray No. 1 is five inches in depth and is subdivided into three compartments. One compartment is intended for stationery, the two others for miscellaneous articles, as enumerated in the subjoined list:

TRAY NO. 1 OF MEDICINE CHEST.

COMPARTMENT A contains—

Paper, cap, ruled, Quire 1.
Paper, Quarto-post, ruled. Quire 1.
Paper, note, ruled, Quire 1.
Envelopes, official, large, No. 25.
Envelopes, official, small. No. 25.
Inkstand, traveller's, filled, No. 1.
Pencils, lead, Faber's, No. 2, No. 6.
Pens. Gillott's steel, No. 12.
Penholders. No. 6.
Ink, carmine, bottles, 1.
Mucilage, bottles, 1.
Elastic rubber-bands, doz., 1.
Pocket register for patients, No. 1.

COMPARTMENT B contains—

Pill Tile, 8 by 6, No. 1.
Probang, No. 1.
Ichthyocolla plaster, in case, yards, 1.
Fountain syringe in case, No. 1.
Assorted corks, box, 1.
Pill Boxes, paper, No. 1.
Matches, in tin box, boxes, 1.

COMPARTMENT C contains—

Brass Spirit Lamp, with wicking, No. 1.
Hard Rubber penis syringe, No. 1.
Tape measure, No. 1.
Suspensory Bandages, No. 6.
Needle-case, filled, No. 1.
Pins, papers, 1.
Tape, roll, 1.

Tray No. 2, of the same dimensions as Tray No. 1, is subdivided into forty-one compartments, and is intended for medicines and such pharmaceutical appliance as are necessary to fit out a temporary dispensary for the field.

TRAY NO. 2, OF MEDICINE CHEST.

THIS TRAY contains—

Extractum Hyoscyami, in 1 oz. pots. oz. 2.
Extractum Conii, in 1 oz. pots, oz. 2.
Extractum Belladonnæ, in 1 oz. pots, oz. 2.
Sodæ Bicarbonas, oz. 6.
Ipecacuanhæ pulvis, oz. 4.
Pilulæ Extracti Colocynth, Comp. (gr. iii.) et Ipecacuanhæ, gr. ss. } No. 500.
Pilulæ Catharticæ Compositæ, No. 600.
Pilulæ Opii, No. 500.
Pilulæ Opii et Camphoræ, No. 500.
Pinliuilæ Quæ Sulphatis (3 grains each) No. 600.
Pilulæ Hydrargyri, oz. 8.
Acidum Tannicum, oz. 4.
Calomel.
Acidum Salicylicum, oz. 4.
Chloral Hydrate, oz. 4.
Rhei pulvis, oz 4.
Acaciæ pulvis, oz. 4.
Plumbi Acetas, oz. 4.
Potassæ Permanganas, oz. 4.

Zinci Sulphas, oz. 2.
Zinci Oxidum, oz. 4.
Morphiæ Sulphas, oz. ½.
Cupri Sulphas, oz. 1.
Argenti Nitras (fused), oz. 1.
Bismuthi Subnitras, oz. 4.
Collodion, oz. 2.
Glycerina, oz. 4.
Ferri Perchloridum, oz. 1.
Tinctura Catechu, oz. 4.
Porcelain Table and Teaspoon, No. 1.
Minim Glass, No. 1.
Hypodermic Syringe, No. 1.
Prescription scales and weights in case, No. 1.
Mortar and pestle, Wedgewood, 3 inch, No. 1.
Spatulæ (large and small), No. 2.
Stethoscope, No. 1.
Scarificator, No. 1.
Scissors, No. 1.
Medicine Glass and Case, No. 1.
Corkscrew, No. 1.

The small half spaces are left for the convenience of packing any small articles which may be considered of importance.

Tray No. 3 is six inches in depth, the other dimensions are similar to the preceding. The bottles used in both trays are eight, four, and two ounce tincture and saltmouths.

TRAY NO. 3 OF MEDICINE CHEST.

Linimentum (as per Standard Supply Table) oz. 8.
Aquæ Ammoniæ, oz. 8.
Spiritus ætheris nitrici, oz. 8.
Tinctura ferri chloridi, oz. 8.
Extractum gentianæ fluidum, oz. 8.
Tinctura Opii, oz. 8.
Chloroformum, oz. 8.
Oleum Terebinthinæ, oz. 8.
Oleum Ricini, oz. 8.
Spiritus Ammoniæ Aromaticus, oz. 8.
Extractum Zingiberis fluidum, oz. 8.
Cough Mixture (per Standard Supply Table) oz. 8.
Tinctura Aconiti Radicis, oz. 8.
Potassæ Chloras, oz. 8.
Potassii Bromidum, oz. 8.

Potassii Iodidum, oz. 8.
Pulvis Ipecacuanhæ et opii, oz. 8.
Quiniæ Sulphas, oz. 8.
Extractum Ergotæ Fluidum, oz. 4.
Extractum Ipecacuanhæ Fluidum, oz. 4.
Spiritus Ætheris Compositus, oz. 4.
Acidum Carbolicum, crystals, oz. 4.
Acidum Aceticum, oz. 4.
Linimentum Cantharides, oz. 4.
Acidum Sulphuricum, oz. 4.
Acidum Nitricum, oz. 4.
Liquor Potassæ, oz. 4.
Cupping Glasses, No. 6.
Clinical Thermometer in case, No. 1.
Urinometer in case, No. 1.
Spaces for powders.

Tray No. 4, of the same length and breadth as the preceding, and eight inches deep, is not subdivided into compartments, and is designed for an assortment of miscellaneous articles.

TRAY NO. 4 OF MEDICINE CHEST.

THE TRAY contains—

Unguentum Hydrargyri, cans, 1.
Ceratum Simplex, cans, 1.
Extractum Nucis Vomicæ, oz. 1.

Vials, prescription, assorted, doz. 1.
Trusses, single, No. 2.
Hard Rubber Syringe, 12 oz., No. 1.

Castile Soap, lbs. 1.
Brown Soap, lbs. 2.
Candles, Sperm, lbs. 4.
Candlesticks, No. 2.
Nutmegs, oz. 2.
Sinapisms, prepared, package, 1.

Sponge, fine pieces, doz. ½.
Portfolio, No. 1.
Towels, doz. 1.
Muslin, yards, 6.
Red flannel, yards, 2.

Tray No. 5, of the same superficial dimensions as the others and eight inches deep, is devoted to hospital stores.

TRAY NO. 5 OF MEDICINE CHEST.

THE TRAY contains—

Spiritus Vini Gallici, oz. 24.
Spiritus Frumenti, oz. 24.
Spiritus Rectificatus, oz. 24.
Oleum Olivæ, oz. 12.
Syrupus Scillæ, oz. 12.

One tin can for Magnesiæ Sulphas.
One tin can for Pulvis Lini.
One tin can for White Sugar.
Two spaces left to be filled at discretion.

MESS CHEST.

The mess chest has been furnished with such utensils as are commonly on hand at every post, and is intended to supply the wants of a temporary field hospital for twelve patients. It has a set of three black walnut trays, each twelve inches wide and sixteen inches long, fitting one above another. The remainder of the chest is left vacant for packing the larger utensils.

Tray No. 1 is four inches in depth and is subdivided.

TRAY NO. 1 OF MESS CHEST.

THIS TRAY contains—

Knives, table, No. 12.
Knives, carving, No. 1.
Forks, table, No. 12.
Forks, carving, No. 1.
Spoons, table, No. 12.
Spoons, tea, No. 12.

Nutmeg grater, No. 1.
Plates, tin, doz. 1.
Pepper box, No. 1.
Salt box, No. 1.
Tin case for matches, No. 1.

Tray No. 2 of the mess chest is five inches in depth, and, designed for cans and packages of various sizes, is not divided into compartments.

TRAY NO. 2 OF MESS CHEST.

This Tray is intended to be packed with extract of beef in cans or jars, condensed milk in cans, farina in papers, corn-starch in papers, and any other article of nourishment or comfort for the sick which may be regarded as necessary by the medical officer.

Tray No. 3, six inches deep, is divided into compartments and furnished with tin cans.

TRAY NO. 3 OF MESS CHEST.

THIS TRAY contains cans for—

Butter,
Coffee, ground, or green,
Pepper,

Salt,
Sugar,
Tea ; or for any other articles desired.

The large space in the chest unoccupied by the Trays is to be packed with the following articles :

Basin, tin, washstand, No. 2.
Cleaver, No. 1.
Cups, Britannia, No. 12.
Cups, tin (1 qt., 1 pt.), No. 2.
Dippers, assorted, No. 2.

Knives, butchers', No. 1.
Ladles, No. 1.
Lantern, No. 1.
Pans, frying, No. 1.
Pans, sauce, No. 1.

Dishes, tin, No. 6.	Pots, coffee, tin, No. 1.
Grater, large, No. 1.	Pots, tea, tin, No. 1.
Gridiron, No. 1.	Saws, butchers, No. 1.
Kettles, camp, covered, No. 1.	Steelyards, No. 1.
Kettles, tea, iron, No. 1.	Trays, tin, No. 1.

To secure the articles contained in the mess chest against injury by motion it will be advisable to pack the spaces firmly with oakum, or some yielding and clean material. Oakum is mentioned, from the fact that it is nearly always found at posts, is cleanly, and, in cases of emergency, may be taken into use as a surgical dressing, or to pad splints.

It is believed that everything which can contribute to the well-being of the sick men of a small command in the field has been provided in these chests, so far as space would allow.

www.ingramcontent.com/pod-product-compliance
Lightning Source LLC
Chambersburg PA
CBHW022030080426
42733CB00007B/783